T0004728

PIE MAKER & CO

TOP 100
taste.COM.AU

PIE MAKER & CO

TOP-RATED RECIPES FOR YOUR FAVOURITE KITCHEN GADGETS

HarperCollins*Publishers*

CONTENTS

HELLO!

At Taste HQ, we know how much Australian cooks love a good hack – and a time-saving device. Indeed, when a certain discount department store put a pie maker on its shelves for a mere $29, it was all the encouragement that home cooks across the country needed to add this surprisingly versatile appliance to their kitchen must-have gadget list.

And we get it! Our food team loves the pie maker too, along with its cousins (sausage roll maker, jaffle maker, waffle maker and air fryer) and we have had so much fun experimenting with them all – Wagon Wheel Cookies anyone? And we've

lost count of how many of our pie maker recipes have gone viral. Not just for pies any more, it really is amazing what you can cook in these clever gadgets!

Of course, it's not just about fun – all of these appliances are incredibly practical as well. Affordable to buy, easy to clean and super fast, they turn out professional-looking food that looks restaurant and cafe-worthy, despite being super simple. And, as always, we've made it easy and affordable by using supermarket ingredients in all our recipes. Every recipe is tried, tested, trusted and rated by the millions of people who use and review taste.com.au every month.

This clever new book has all our favourite creations, along with expert tips and hacks from our food team. Take the journey with us into *Pie Maker & Co* and we promise that you will save time, effort – and bring a little fun back into your everyday cooking.

Brodee

**BRODEE MYERS,
EDITOR-IN-CHIEF**

HOW TO USE
PIE MAKER & CO

Welcome to taste.com.au's *Pie Maker & Co*, with all the recipes, tips and healthy hacks you need to create magic with your favourite kitchen appliances.

AMAZING FEATURES

Full prep & cooking times

Complete nutritional information

5-star recipe ratings

At-a-glance prep times

Reviews from home cooks

KEY GUIDES
Highlighted dots indicating freezable, kid friendly, make ahead, speedy and vego

COOK'S TIPS
Helpful hints and insider knowledge courtesy of our expert food team

SWAP IT OUT

Our ingredient swaps add variety, save time, or adapt for dietary needs.

SWAP IT OUT

Use hoisin sauce instead of barbecue to give this dish an Asian twist.

CRUNCH THE NUMBERS

Make informed meal choices for you and your family using nutritional panels. They help you track your calories and calculate your protein, carbs and fat.

NUTRITION (PER SERVE)

CAL	FAT	SAT FAT	PROTEIN	CARBS
216	7g	2g	14g	18g

INFO AT A GLANCE

Use the icons to find the best choices for you and your family (such as freezable, kid friendly, make ahead, speedy and vego – or all five at once). Just follow the highlighted dots, or turn to our index, which starts on page 246.

● FREEZABLE ● KID FRIENDLY ● MAKE AHEAD ● SPEEDY ● VEGO

THE BASICS

We all love a gadget, but it needs to work for you – not gather dust inside a kitchen cupboard. We show you how to make the most of the clever appliances used in this book. You will be surprised by what you can create with them!

THE TASTE.COM.AU GUARANTEE

All taste.com.au recipes are triple-tested, rated and reviewed by Aussie cooks just like you. Plus, every ingredient is as close as your local supermarket.

GETTING STARTED

EXPERT TIPS, TRICKS AND HACKS ON HOW TO MAKE THESE CLEVER DEVICES WORK FOR YOU.

THE BASICS

We all love a gadget, but it needs to work – not gather dust inside a kitchen cupboard. Here are our tips for making the most of these clever appliances.

CHOOSE THE RIGHT APPLIANCE FOR YOU

Do your research. Before you head to the shops, take time to think about how your family cooks – and your usual weekly meal schedule. Be honest with yourself before parting with your hard-earned cash.

Preparing lots of lunch box treats? The pie maker could make your life easier. Want to get healthier with your evening meals? Look to the air fryer, which will help you minimise how much fat you are using. Waffle makers are great for families who enjoy leisurely weekend brunches – or they are a useful addition to a holiday home or caravan.

Not sure if you want to invest a lot of money in an appliance and then have it buried at the back of the cupboard, never seeing the light of day? Consider heading to Aldi, Kmart or Target, who all have budget ranges, and try their offerings out first. If it becomes a staple of your kitchen, you can then invest in some of the more premium brands, whose products may last longer and have more features.

MAKE THEM KID-FRIENDLY

One of the best things about pie makers, sausage roll makers and jaffle makers is that they are kid-friendly. School-aged children can easily make their own after-school snacks or treats with minimal adult intervention. It's an ideal way of getting them comfortable in the kitchen – and the short cooking time gives just the right amount of reward before they lose interest!

Take your kids through how the appliances work – showing them the safety features along the way.

Some parents even prepare mixtures for the pie maker the night before, leaving them refrigerated for teens to help themselves when they get home after school. Simple and effective! And a great confidence booster for novice cooks.

Air fryers are safer for teens and older children to use than deep-fryers because they don't use loads of hot oil, which can be dangerous to handle. While younger kids should still be supervised when using an air fryer, they are a great, safer way of heating up leftovers.

CARING FOR YOUR APPLIANCE

It might go without saying, but it's best to let your appliance cool and then give it a quick wipe over before you place it back in the cupboard. Do this every time you use it. This will make sure that bits of food are not caught inside, where they can rot over time (especially if you only use the gadget occasionally).

Most of the appliances used in this book are coated with a non-stick finish, which, while great for maintenance, does need special handling. Clean cooled appliances with hot, soapy water using a sponge or dishcloth. Never submerge an electrical appliance in water – always clean them on the benchtop. For appliances with leftover oil or food residue, cleaning pads labelled safe for non-stick cookware and bakeware can be used with standard dishwashing liquid.

Clean air fryers after every use, including the basket, the drawer that collects any oil or drippings, and the machine itself. A sign that your air fryer has oil build-up and is due for a good clean is if you notice smoke starting to come out of your machine when you use it.

The outside of your appliance usually needs just a quick wipe with a damp kitchen cloth if there are any accidental drips or splashes on it.

Give it a quick wipe over before you place it back in the cupboard. Do this every time you use it.

School-aged children can easily make after-school snacks or treats with minimal adult intervention.

EASY AS PIE

Home cooks are now finding new ways to use pie makers. From fast fritters to deliciously gooey doughnuts, this is the new way to cook.

WHAT WE LOVE ABOUT IT

Often for sale around $30 (the Kmart version went viral), the pie maker has had a huge resurgence in popularity in recent years. Online groups have formed to chat, share tips and recipes, and taste.com.au members have embraced this old-but-new way of cooking. No longer just for traditional meat or fruit pies, this clever appliance works with all sorts of mixtures, turning out everything from super-simple frittatas and quiches to doughnuts and muffins.

And because it usually takes 12-15 minutes for your goodies to be ready, the rewards can be almost instant!

WHAT YOU NEED TO KNOW

There are a few pie makers on the market, ranging in cost from $29 to about $80, depending on the brand and the size of the unit. The more expensive models often come with pastry cutters to make preparing pies even easier. They usually create four pies, but there are six-pie versions available, as well as single family-sized pie options.

It's important to make a note of the size of the moulds in your maker: some brands are quite generous in the sizing, which makes the finished product suitable for main meals; others are better for breakfasts and snacks. Our pie maker recipes have been designed for the smaller four-hole pie maker with a volume of about 80ml (⅓ cup) in each hole, so you may need to adjust the quantities to suit your appliance.

Most pie makers have a non-stick surface, which means they are super-easy to clean – all they usually need is just a wipe over with a damp cloth after use.

HOW IT WORKS

The big benefit of the pie maker is how quickly they cook! They usually only take 12-15 minutes, depending on pastry and filling – with no more waiting for the oven to heat.

If you are using pastry to enclose your pie, we recommend you pre-cook the fillings before using the pie maker – or even reheat pre-cooked fillings (such as leftovers) to ensure they are warmed through.

TOP 10 IDEAS

1 PIES
Let's start with the obvious. The pie maker can, of course, make you four perfect pies. Use shortcrust or puff pastry, add filling (sweet or savoury), pop on a lid and voila! See p24 for pastry recipes.

2 VEGIE SLICE
This kid-friendly favourite can be in the lunchbox in 20 minutes! Mix vegies and egg in a bowl (zucchini is always a winner) and spoon into the pie maker.

3 DOUGHNUTS
Jam, cherry, Nutella, cinnamon, you name it, and someone has tried to make it in this little timesaver. Aussie home cooks have truly embraced the pie maker doughnut.

4 MAC 'N' CHEESE
What better way to spend Sunday than whipping up a pot of mac 'n' cheese, adding it to the pie maker and crisping it into little pies? Comfort food at its best.

5 EGGS
Whip up brekkie favourites in no time. Try cracking an egg inside a rasher of bacon, or quickly poach by leaving the lid open.

6 TORTILLAS
These Mexican standbys are easily adapted to the pie maker. Fill with taco sauce, mince and/or beans and enclose them for a midweek meal.

7 MUFFINS
Raspberry, chocolate chip or vanilla, whatever muffin flavour takes your fancy. The pie maker can even create delicious treats such lemon tarts.

8 POTATOES
Whether creating hash browns, or a delicious base for a quick snack, grated or mashed potato is pure pie maker heaven.

9 PANCAKES
These indulgent breakfast staples are easy to whip up in the pie maker. Try adding fruit to the mixture – blueberries are perfect.

10 BREAD
With its simple functionality and even heat, many bread and scone recipes can be adapted for the pie maker – adjust your favourite!

This clever appliance works with all sorts of mixtures.

Sausage roll makers used to be more of a secret (almost cult) appliance, but their rising popularity has left us wondering what we ever did without them.

ON A ROLL

Hot on the heels of its more famous relative, the pie maker,
the sausage roll maker has become the latest kitchen must-have.

WHAT WE LOVE ABOUT IT

Sausage roll makers (SRMs) have built their most ardent fans through the use of sweet and indulgent fillings. So, while some people are making actual sausage rolls in the sausage roll maker, the bulk of the fun seems to involve desserts and cakes. Brownies, doughnuts, finger buns, eclairs and apple pies can all be made in the sausage roll maker... you will start to see the attraction. They are ideal for whipping up a last-minute dessert for unexpected guests, or a midweek sweet surprise for the family.

WHAT YOU NEED TO KNOW

Like the pie maker, the sausage roll maker has been a hit with home cooks because of its ease of use and versatility. While not quite hitting the sales hype of the pie maker, it really moved into the mainstream when Kmart released its bargain version. With more Australians battling food intolerances, the sausage roll maker also allows you to control the ingredients to meet your family's dietary needs. They work well with gluten-free and dairy-free ingredients, and it's easy to whip up some vegan delicacies too!

HOW IT WORKS

Sausage roll makers used to be more of a secret (almost cult) appliance and hard to find in homeware stores, but their rising popularity has meant that many more options are now available. We know that Australian home cooks love a gadget hack and, in consequence, the shelves are filling in major electronic outlets as a number of well-known brands rush to launch their own versions of these nifty appliances. Easy to clean, quick to cook with, they usually have a non-stick surface and just need a quick wipe down with a clean kitchen cloth after use.

The sausage roll maker allows you to control ingredients to meet your family's dietary needs.

TOP 10 IDEAS

1 SAUSAGE ROLLS

This appliance makes these snacks simple and speedy. Go traditional with a cooked mince filling using different flavour combos such as lamb and mint, pork and veal, or leftover bolognaise.

2 MARS BARS

In a delicious twist, full-sized Mars Bars fit perfectly into the sausage roll maker. Encase them in sweet puff pastry and you have a rich and gooey dessert in less than 15 minutes.

3 CHEESE AND SPINACH PASTRIES

These vegetarian standbys are easy to whip up and always a crowd pleaser. Go kid-friendly and choose tasty cheese, or add tang with a blue or goat's cheese.

4 BROWNIES

These easy-to-mix, crowd-friendly baked goodies are a cinch in the sausage roll maker. Try classic chocolate, or even a blondie, with a vanilla base.

5 GOZLEME

These school fete favourites are perfect in the sausage roll maker! Like most bread-based goodies, they cook evenly, allowing you to enjoy them hot.

6 LASAGNE

Sausage roll maker lasagne rolls have all your favourite flavours in one easy recipe. With or without béchamel sauce, they are a winner.

7 DOUGHNUTS

We've made some incredible jam and cream doughnuts in an SRM. Make your own batter, or use a supermarket doughnut or pancake mix.

8 PIES

Fruit pies are ideally suited to the cylindrical shape of the sausage roll maker: try apple or blueberry for a classic sweet snack.

9 PANCAKES

Create super-fast filled pancakes. The perfect brekkie after a kids sleepover, it keeps mess to a minimum, and flavour to the max.

10 HALOUMI

This tangy and salty cheese keeps its shape when heated, making it perfect for a quick carb-free snack, or add some mountain bread to make it more filling.

LIGHT AS AIR

Air fryers are one of the fastest selling kitchen appliances in store today.
Healthy, speedy and easy to use, it's no wonder they are so popular.

WHAT WE LOVE ABOUT IT

Australians are going wild for air fryer recipes right now and it's easy to understand why. They're simple to use, cook things in a matter of minutes and you can get very similar results to deep-frying, with much less oil. Indeed, some appliance manufacturers claim that the maximum oil you will ever need is one tablespoon when cooking from scratch – and nothing at all if you are reheating prepared foods. This makes them a healthy way to enjoy the foods you love.

WHAT YOU NEED TO KNOW

Air fryers can be used instead of a deep fryer, or for recipes that would traditionally call for baking in an oven. While an air fryer still needs some oil (a spray of oil is often all that's required), it uses up to 80 per cent less oil than deep frying. This means that your kitchen doesn't get as hot – and it's much safer because you won't be lifting heavy pans of boiling oil when cooking or draining food. Cleaning is usually pretty easy and many manufacturers have designed the baskets to be dishwasher-friendly. Make sure you give your air fryer a quick rinse after every use.

HOW IT WORKS

Air fryers work in a similar way to a fan-forced oven, by circulating heated air around food that is placed in a basket, accessed either using a pull-out drawer or top lid. Despite their name, they don't really fry food, but rather heat it evenly using a high-powered fan to circulate hot air. It's important to note that they aren't as fast as deep fryers, and take a similar amount of time as a fan-forced oven to deliver their baked goodies. Capacity ranges from about 1.5 to 7.3 litres. Check the box for working or cooking capacity, if provided. Visit the store to check the size of the air fryer, along with how easy it is to insert and remove the basket.

TOP 10 IDEAS

1 FRIED CHICKEN

The air fryer provides the crunch and none of the grease. Use drumsticks, chicken wings or thigh cutlets to create this fast food favourite and conquer that craving! You can even toss them in some chilli salt for an extra kick.

2 PUFF PASTRY TARTS

The air fryer is ideal for simple tarts and can have them ready in less than 30 minutes. Just use store-bought frozen pastry and top with your favourites – cherry tomatoes and goat's cheese is a simple and easy combo, or try pan-fried mushrooms and blue cheese.

3 SCHNITZEL

Whether you go for the traditional chicken or veal, or a vegie option such as sweet potato or cauliflower, the air fryer can cook this classic pub favourite quickly and without much mess. Top with melted cheese for the ultimate in deliciousness.

4 FISH AND CHIPS

The air fryer could have been designed for this dish! Choose either a traditional batter (try 1 cup SR flour, a pinch of salt and 1 cup soda water or beer), or perhaps a light coating of panko breadcrumbs, as a great option for Friday night.

5 KALE CHIPS

This is the ultimate dish for when you're craving hot chips, but want to be a bit kinder to your body. Simply break kale into pieces, spray with oil and throw into the air fryer basket in a single layer. The perfect snack for when you're binge-watching a TV series!

6 BAKED POTATOES

Who doesn't love a baked spud? And they are so simple in the air fryer. Spray with a light coating of olive oil and sprinkle with sea salt and sprigs of rosemary before baking in your air fryer to create a simple side. This also works well with pumpkin or sweet potato, topped with fresh sage leaves.

As well as cooking great meals from scratch, air fryers are a convenient solution for reheating leftovers or ready-made food.

7 SCONES

Here's a great tip to cater for unexpected guests. Scone dough (so easy!) can be made up and frozen in small batches, ready to be thrown into the air fryer when needed. They cook in just 15 minutes and freezing the mixture helps make them lighter. Serve with whipped cream and jam.

8 GARLIC BREAD

Everyone's favourite bread can be reheated and served warm. Just use a standard baguette, slice almost all the way through and spread between slices with garlic butter before placing in the air fryer to be heated. Serve warm as a side dish.

9 REHEATING LEFTOVERS

The air fryer is a great way to heat leftovers without drying them out. Especially good with breads and pastry (we love warming croissants for an indulgent European-style breakfast), it won't make them soggy or chewy, unlike a microwave.

10 SPRING ROLLS

Store-bought ready-made fried foods are great in the air fryer, creating a quick snack or light meal. Frozen pies, spring rolls, pastizzi or sausage rolls all work well, creating a crispy result with much less fat than a deep fryer. They are also perfect for heating (or reheating) pizzas, as they keep the base crisp.

Why not adapt
your favourite
meal into a toastie?
The combinations
are endless!

TOAST MASTERS

Take your sandwiches to the next level with a fresh look at jaffles and toasties.

WHAT WE LOVE ABOUT IT

Way back in the day, toasted sandwiches were made under the searing heat of a grill, fried in a pan or – for outdoor types – in a cast iron jaffle maker over a camp fire. Then, in the mid 1970s, came a how-did-we-live-without-it gadget that was quite literally, the best thing for (and since) sliced bread. And because it usually takes between 12-15 minutes for your goodies to be ready, the rewards can be almost instant!

WHAT YOU NEED TO KNOW

The jaffle maker has come a long way and now varies in size and features. Some of the budget offerings are super affordable, but may not be large enough for a standard slice of bread, while premium offerings can include deep pockets if you love generous fillings. A Teflon coating will allow for easy cleaning, and look for one with an in-built cutting tool, to make jaffles easier to serve. A sandwich press, which uses flat iron hot plates instead of enclosed parcels of the standard jaffle maker, is also an option.

HOW IT WORKS

Features such as "floating hinges" and "adjustable plate heights" allow us to whip up everything from wafer-thin quesadillas to open sandwich melts. Add to that the variety of bread now available – rye, soy and linseed, Turkish, mountain, sourdough, panini, spelt, even plain old sliced white – and you can be the toastie with the mostie. When you are using your appliance (jaffle maker or sandwich press), it's best not to use bread slices that are any thicker than 1.5cm or 2cm at the most, otherwise it's only the bread that toasts, and not the fillings you have added.

TOP 10 IDEAS

1 HAM AND CHEESE

It might sound obvious, but better-than-average ham and better-than-average cheese on better-than-average bread make a better sandwich. Croque monsieur, anyone? In other words, spend the extra on ingredients and reap the delicious rewards.

2 PICKLED VEGIES

Fresh vegetables are best avoided in toasties as they don't have time to develop their flavour. Try pickled vegetables such as sauerkraut, roasted eggplant, capsicum or sweet potato, and semi or sun-dried tomatoes.

3 FRUITS

It's easy to forget about sweet toasties, but they can be a surprisingly delicious dessert. Try preserved, canned or frozen fruit inside sweet bread such as brioche, panettone or raisin toast. Dust with icing sugar.

4 RELISHES AND PICKLES

These tangy sides are great condiment choices in a jaffle. If you need something to bind it together, go for a little finely grated cheese.

5 BREAKFAST

Return to the old favourite of a BLAT (bacon, lettuce, avo and tomato) for a classic start to the day.

6 ITALIAN STYLE

The Italians are famous for their focaccia. Take their lead and toast deli meats such as salami, mortadella or prosciutto and top with semi-dried tomato.

7 CHEESE

Grated cheese will melt faster than thick slices. This is especially important if you want the heat to do its work on all the ingredients.

8 HEATED FILLINGS

Some jaffle fillings – stewed meat or baked beans as a vego option – benefit from being heated a little first.

9 EXTRA ZING

Finely chopped raw white onion puts a zing into a toastie. Especially good with tuna and strong cheddar.

10 GET CREATIVE

Why not adapt your favourite meal into a toastie? The combinations are endless – lasagne toastie (with oozing béchamel sauce), pulled pork, Mexican beef.

WAFFLING ON

Surprisingly versatile, these clever gadgets can turn out restaurant-quality breakfasts, brunches and lunches.

WHAT WE LOVE ABOUT IT

What is there not to love about waffles, with their crispy outside encasing a fluffy, soft interior? Prices for waffle makers start at about $30, ranging up to $180 for all the bells and whistles. And with a huge range on sale, you can decide on different sizes, shapes and depth, depending on how you like your waffles. Thinner waffles cook quickly and work with simple sauces and toppings, while the deeper dishes will help to create a Belgian-style waffle, which is thicker and fluffier.

WHAT YOU NEED TO KNOW

Not just for sweet treats, you can adapt waffle batter mixtures to create savoury lunches and variations on fritters. As well, different waffle press shapes are available – round, square or even heart shaped – so you can choose whichever shape you like best. Most waffle makers create four waffles at a time, so it can be a bit of a slow procedure if you're feeding a crowd. When you are making a large batch, keep the first waffles warm in a low oven while you cook the rest. It's usually best to heat the waffle maker first before filling it with your chosen batter mixture.

HOW IT WORKS

Designed to be super-easy, simply whip up a quick batter – sweet or savoury – and pour it in to cook. Latest models cook waffles more evenly, making them almost foolproof. Some brands of waffle maker include LCD displays that allow you to choose the type of waffle you are cooking for more accurate results. Choose from Belgian, classic, chocolate, buttermilk or custom. Many waffle makers also have a spill zone for excess batter that stops the overflow from catching and burning.

TOP 10 IDEAS

1 BERRIES
The classic combo, fresh mixed berries are made for waffles. Serve strawberries and blueberries scattered over the top with a dusting of icing sugar. You can also blend them into a coulis and drizzle them on top.

2 BANANA AND HONEY
This duo is a match made in heaven. Slightly warm the honey so it flows freely over the hot waffle.

3 CORN
Go for a café-style brekkie with a savoury cornbread waffle, topped with bacon and avocado.

4 HONEYCOMB BUTTER
Take inspiration from Bill Granger: top your waffle with butter blended with honeycomb and watch it melt into the crevices.

5 ICE-CREAM
Ice-cream is perfect when paired with still-warm waffles. Vanilla is always a winner, although a quality chocolate ice-cream adds an element of luxury.

6 POTATO
Grated potato (think hash browns) makes a perfect base for savoury waffles. Top with baby spinach leaves, or serve on its own as a side.

Not just for sweet treats, you can adapt waffle batter mixtures to create savoury lunches and fritters.

7 NUTELLA

Everyone's favourite spread, this is delicious on a warm waffle and topped with banana and crushed nuts.

8 CAULIFLOWER

Perfect for the gluten-intolerant, use grated cauliflower as the base of a waffle-style fritter and top with roasted truss tomatoes and scattered basil leaves.

9 SMASHED AVO

Use waffles to make a fun version of this café stalwart. Add julienned green apple and ginger for a tangy twist.

10 WAFFLE STACK

Line them up and sandwich waffle pieces with vanilla cream for a special dessert. Drizzle with chocolate syrup.

ALL ABOUT PASTRY

While it's always good to have some store-bought pastry in the freezer for last-minute guests or fast meals, it's not difficult to make your own.

WHAT YOU NEED TO KNOW

If you are the proud owner of a pie or sausage roll maker, be prepared to work with pastry frequently. So many delicious goodies can be the result of that magic combination of flour, eggs and butter! So whether you are preparing a family meat pie, indulgent chocolate eclairs or even just a quick snack for the kids, here are our insider tips on the main types of pastry – shortcrust, puff, filo and choux – and how to make each of them.

HOW TO USE

Shortcrust is a great all-rounder and the best for pies and tarts. **Puff pastry** is lighter and fluffier, with a buttery texture, and is often used as the top of a pie or to wrap a sausage roll. Found in many Greek and Middle Eastern dishes, **filo** can be a little fiddly to make yourself, but it's so much fun! Beloved by the French and used in such delicacies as chocolate eclairs and profiteroles, **choux** pastry is easy to make – and it's all done on the stovetop.

PASTRY RECIPES

SHORTCRUST

For a basic shortcrust recipe, process 250g (1⅔ cups) plain flour, 125g butter and a pinch of salt in a food processor until the mixture resembles breadcrumbs. Whisk 1 egg and 1 tablespoon chilled water in a bowl until combined, then with food processor motor running, add to flour mixture. Process until mixture begins to form large clumps, stopping machine before mixture forms a ball. Turn pastry out onto a work surface and knead gently to bring together. Form into a disc for a round tart or into a log shape for a rectangular tart. Wrap in plastic wrap and refrigerate overnight or for at least 2 hours.

For sweet shortcrust, add 80g sifted icing sugar with the flour and replace egg with 2 egg yolks.

PUFF PASTRY

Sift 250g (1⅔ cups) strong (baker's) flour into a large bowl with a good pinch of sea salt. Add 250g chopped unsalted butter to the flour and rub in using your hands. You should still be able to see chunks of butter. Make a well in the centre, add 100ml cold water and combine, adding a little more water if necessary, until you have a firm rough dough. Roll out on a lightly floured board into a rectangle measuring about 20cm x 50cm. You should be able to see streaks of butter in the pastry. Fold a third of the pastry into the centre, then fold the bottom third up over that. Give the folded dough a quarter turn and roll it out again. Repeat the process of folding, rolling and turning twice more. Chill pastry for 30 minutes before rolling out again and using.

FILO

Combine 500g (2 cups) plain flour, 250ml (1 cup) water and ¼ teaspoon salt in a bowl. Mix until dough comes together. Turn onto a lightly floured surface and knead until smooth, adding more flour if too sticky. Place in a lightly oiled bowl, cover with plastic wrap and rest for 1 hour. Divide into eight pieces and feed each piece through a pasta machine, dusting with flour and reducing settings until the dough is about 4mm thick. Gently stretch filo sheets with your hands, pulling from the edges until almost transparent (this is the bit that takes practice). Brush each with melted butter, placing baking paper between pastry sheets to prevent them sticking. Wrap tightly with plastic wrap and refrigerate until required. Bring to room temperature before using.

CHOUX

Combine 60g butter and 185ml (⅔ cup) cold water in a saucepan over medium heat. Cook for 3-4 minutes until butter has melted and mixture just starts to boil. Reduce heat to low. Add 100g (⅔ cup) plain flour. Cook, stirring, for 2-3 minutes until mixture comes away from side of pan and forms a ball. Cool slightly. Using a wooden spoon, gradually beat in 3 lightly whisked eggs until well combined and dough is glossy. Choux doesn't need to be chilled or rolled. Place it in a resealable plastic bag, cut off one corner and squeeze it into the pie maker holes.

Here are our insider tips on the main types of pastry — and how to make each of them.

5 PASTRY FLAVOUR HACKS

1 VANILLA BEAN
Add the scraped seeds of a vanilla bean, or 2 teaspoons of vanilla paste, to shortcrust pastry for extra aromatic sweetness. Perfect for fruit pies.

2 SOUR CREAM
Sour cream can add a tang to pastry bases. Process 300g (2 cups) plain flour with 200g chilled butter until it resembles breadcrumbs. Add 130g (½ cup) sour cream and process until it forms a smooth ball. Wrap in plastic wrap and chill for an hour before using in your favourite recipe.

3 SAGE
Add 2 tablespoons of chopped sage to shortcrust pastry for a flavour boost in savoury tarts and pies. Sage is a great match for pumpkin or zucchini.

4 CHOCOLATE
Place 190g (1¼ cups) plain flour, 45g (¼ cup) sifted icing sugar and 30g (¼ cup) cocoa powder in a food processor. Process until just combined. Add 100g butter. Pulse until the mixture resembles fine breadcrumbs. Add 2½ tablespoons iced water and process until the mixture just starts to clump together (add a little extra iced water if needed). This recipe makes enough chocolate pastry for a family-sized flan.

5 PARMESAN
This tangy cheese adds a bite to savoury tarts. Follow the basic shortcrust pastry recipe, adding 50g finely grated parmesan with the flour. For toppings, think ricotta and spinach, or feta, semi-dried tomatoes and olives.

PERFECT PASTRY TOP TIPS

The foodies at taste.com.au have a few tricks up their sleeve to help you get the most out of the pastry you make for your pie maker.

FLOUR POWER
Lightly dust your work surface and the rolling pin with flour. Don't use too much flour or it can alter the texture of the pastry. Roll the pastry out with even pressure in one direction, turning it 90 degrees between each roll. When turning the pastry, lightly throw a little flour under it as you go to stop it sticking to the bench.

CUTTING PASTRY
When cutting and trimming pastry, use a sharp knife that cuts quickly and cleanly without dragging. If your pie maker has a pastry cutter, lightly dust it with flour and cut firmly into the pastry. Don't wiggle the cutter – this results in an unclean, jagged edge. To easily remove each pastry disc from the bench, use a metal egg slide dusted with flour to remove the disc in one clean motion, keeping a neat, even shape.

BUTTER UP
When making pastry, use cold butter from the fridge so that your pastry is firm and easy to handle.

JUST CHILL
Allow time for chilling or resting the dough before you roll it out. The butter will have softened during mixing, and chilling allows it to firm up again so the pastry won't be greasy. Chilling also allows the gluten in the flour to relax, which helps prevent the pastry from shrinking and cracking in the pie maker.

DON'T OVERWORK
Roll and handle dough (especially puff pastry) as little as possible: overworking it can make pastry tough instead of light and crisp.

FREEZE IT
Double the quantities of our shortcrust, puff and filo pastry recipes and freeze half to use later.

ONE AT A TIME
When assembling pies in the pie maker, work with one pie hole at a time, or the pastry will start to dry out and become brittle.

LEFTOVERS
Wrap leftover cooled pies in plastic wrap and freeze for up to 3 months.

★★★★★

I have never made a meat pie in my life & I do a lot of baking. Since I have had my pie maker, the satisfaction of doing it yourself & it working is brilliant. **RAYLON**

PIE MAKER

USE THIS CLEVER AND VERSATILE GADGET
FOR EVERYTHING FROM MEAT PIES
TO SWEET TREATS AND SPEEDY SNACKS.

CARAMILK CUSTARD DOUGHNUTS

The pie maker takes the fuss out of making fresh, hot custard-filled doughnuts for a family-friendly sweet treat.

MAKES 12 **PREP** 20 mins (+ chilling) **COOK** 30 mins

150g (1 cup) self-raising flour
2 tbs cocoa powder, sifted
2 tbs caster sugar, plus 70g (⅓ cup)
    extra for sprinkling
185ml (¾ cup) milk
2 eggs, lightly beaten
90g butter, melted, cooled, plus
    60g extra for brushing

CARAMILK CUSTARD FILLING
1 tbs custard powder
125ml (½ cup) milk
75g Cadbury Caramilk
    chocolate, chopped

1 For the filling, place custard powder in a small saucepan. Add 1 tablespoon milk. Stir until smooth. Add remaining milk. Stir to combine. Cook over medium-high heat, stirring, for 2-3 minutes until mixture boils and thickens. Remove from heat. Stir in chocolate until melted and smooth. Transfer to a heatproof bowl. Cover surface with plastic wrap. Set aside for 5 minutes to cool. Refrigerate for 15 minutes or until set.

2 Meanwhile, combine flour, cocoa and sugar in a large bowl. Whisk milk and eggs in a jug until combined. Make a well in centre of flour mixture. Add egg mixture and butter. Stir until just combined.

3 Preheat a pie maker. Working quickly, spoon 1 tablespoon doughnut mixture into each hole. Quickly spoon 2 teaspoons custard into centre of each hole. Cover each with 1 tablespoon doughnut mixture. Close lid. Cook for 9 minutes or until doughnuts spring back when lightly touched. Carefully transfer to a wire rack set over a tray. Brush tops with extra butter. Sprinkle with extra sugar.

4 Repeat process to make 12 doughnuts. Serve warm or at room temperature.

COOK'S TIP

Swap the Caramilk chocolate for milk or dark chocolate if you prefer.

NUTRITION (EACH)

CALS	FAT	SAT FAT	PROTEIN	CARBS
229	14g	9g	3.8g	23g

○ FREEZABLE ○ KID FRIENDLY ○ MAKE AHEAD ○ SPEEDY ● VEGO

★★★★★ *These turned out great,
super easy to make.* **LITTLEENGLAND**

PINA COLADA TARTS

Tropical fruit and a splash of rum really make these dessert treats.
Try them as a snack with coffee or served with ice-cream after dinner.

MAKES 8 **PREP** 15 mins **COOK** 20 mins

1 egg, separated, plus extra 1 yolk
70g (⅓ cup) caster sugar
35g (½ cup) shredded coconut
432g can pineapple chunks in juice
80g butter, softened
2 tbs plain flour
1½ tbs white rum
2 sheets frozen puff pastry,
  slightly thawed

1 Whisk the egg white with 2 tablespoons sugar in a large bowl until frothy. Add the coconut. Stir to combine. Drain pineapple over a medium saucepan to catch juice. Chop the pineapple chunks.

2 Place butter and both egg yolks in a medium bowl. Whisk until smooth and combined. Add flour, two-thirds of the coconut mixture and 2 teaspoons of rum. Whisk until combined.

3 Preheat a pie maker. Using the pie-maker base cutter, cut 8 large rounds from pastry sheets. Place 4 rounds into the pie maker. Quickly divide half the batter between pastry shells. Top with half the pineapple. Sprinkle over half the remaining coconut mixture. Close lid. Cook for 10 minutes or until pastry is puffed and golden. Transfer to a wire rack. Repeat with remaining pastry, batter, pineapple and coconut mixture to make 8 tarts.

4 Meanwhile, add remaining sugar to reserved pineapple juice. Heat over medium heat. Cook, stirring, for 2 minutes or until sugar dissolves. Increase heat to high. Bring to the boil. Boil, without stirring, for 8 minutes or until syrupy. Remove from heat. Stir in remaining rum. Drizzle syrup over tarts. Serve.

NUTRITION (PER SERVE)

CALS	FAT	SAT FAT	PROTEIN	CARBS
285	17g	11g	3.7g	28g

○ FREEZABLE   ○ KID FRIENDLY   ● MAKE AHEAD   ○ SPEEDY   ● VEGO

SECRET HACK
*If you aren't a fan of pineapple,
consider any canned fruit – peaches or
apricots would work equally well.*

WAGON-WHEEL
COOKIES

Your childhood favourite snack gets a super-easy revamp for the pie maker, and it's ready in under half an hour.

MAKES 12 **PREP** 10 mins (+ chilling) **COOK** 5 mins

24 chocolate ripple biscuits (see tip)
155g (½ cup) raspberry jam (see tip)
9 vanilla marshmallows
100g (½ cup) dark chocolate
   melts, melted

1 Place 12 biscuits flat-side up on a board. Spread each with ¼ teaspoon jam. Using scissors, cut marshmallows into quarters. Top each biscuit with 3 pieces of marshmallow.

2 Preheat a pie maker. Spread remaining biscuits on flat side with remaining jam.

3 Place 4 of the prepared biscuits, marshmallow-side up, into pie maker. Close lid. Cook for 30 seconds or until marshmallow softens. Carefully lift out biscuits and sandwich each with a jam-spread biscuit, pressing to flatten marshmallow. Repeat with remaining biscuits to make 12 wagon wheels.

4 Spoon melted chocolate into a sealable plastic bag. Snip off 1 corner. Drizzle wagon wheels with chocolate. Refrigerate for 10 minutes or until chocolate is set. Serve.

COOK'S TIPS

You'll need a 250g packet of choc ripple biscuits for this recipe. You can make these with any flavoured jam you prefer.

NUTRITION (EACH)

CALS	FAT	SAT FAT	PROTEIN	CARBS
168	4.9g	3.2g	1.4g	28g

○ FREEZABLE ○ KID FRIENDLY ● MAKE AHEAD ● SPEEDY ○ VEGO

★★★★★ *Super easy to make: a fast, fun snack loved by adults and kids alike.* **LEAHO771**

IRISH CREAM BRIOCHE
PUDDINGS

Warning! This is not your grandma's bread-and-butter pudding recipe. Flavoured with a splash of Baileys, these sweet treats will be a huge hit.

MAKES 8 **PREP** 10 mins **COOK** 10 mins

2 eggs
80ml (⅓ cup) Baileys
   Irish Cream liqueur
2 tbs milk
½ x 400g loaf chocolate chip
   brioche, cut into 2.5cm cubes
Whipped cream and cocoa
   powder, to serve

1 Place eggs, Baileys and milk in a large bowl. Whisk until combined. Add brioche. Toss to coat in egg mixture. Set aside for 3 minutes for brioche to soak up liquid.

2 Preheat a pie maker. Divide half the brioche mixture among pie-maker holes. Close the lid. Cook for 4 minutes or until a skewer inserted into the centre of puddings comes out clean. Carefully transfer puddings to a wire rack. Repeat with remaining brioche mixture to make 8 puddings.

3 Serve puddings warm or at room temperature, dolloped with whipped cream and dusted with cocoa.

COOK'S TIP

Use day-old raisin bread instead of brioche if you prefer.

NUTRITION (EACH)

CALS	FAT	SAT FAT	PROTEIN	CARBS
150	7g	3g	4.3g	16g

○ FREEZABLE   ○ KID FRIENDLY   ● MAKE AHEAD   ● SPEEDY   ● VEGO

10 minutes prep

SWAP IT OUT
To make this
alcohol-free, use a
combination of cream
and chocolate syrup
in place of the
Baileys.

SUGAR-CRUST BLUEBERRY PANCAKES

Who said pancakes have to be flat? Spoon fruity batter into a pie maker for a no-fuss, no-mess breakfast option.

MAKES 8 **PREP** 15 mins **COOK** 15 mins

150g (1 cup) self-raising flour
2 tbs caster sugar
½ tsp baking powder
185ml (¾ cup) buttermilk
2 eggs
20g butter, melted
1 tsp finely grated lemon rind
100g (¾ cup) frozen blueberries
60g (⅓ cup) pure icing sugar
1 tsp lemon juice
Raw sugar, to serve

1 Combine the flour, caster sugar and baking powder in a large bowl. Place buttermilk, eggs, butter and lemon rind in a jug. Whisk until combined. Make a well in centre of flour mixture. Add buttermilk mixture. Whisk until just combined. Fold in blueberries.

2 Preheat the pie maker. Spoon enough batter into each hole to reach the rim. Close the lid. Cook for 6 minutes or until puffed and golden. Repeat with remaining batter to make 8 pancakes.

3 Meanwhile, stir icing sugar and lemon juice in a bowl until smooth. Spoon over pancakes and sprinkle with raw sugar to serve.

COOK'S TIP

Substitute any frozen or fresh berries for the blueberries.

NUTRITION (EACH)

CALS	FAT	SAT FAT	PROTEIN	CARBS
162	3.6g	1.9g	4.2g	28g

○ FREEZABLE ○ KID FRIENDLY ○ MAKE AHEAD ● SPEEDY ● VEGO

SWAP IT OUT

*Use gluten-free flour and baking powder to make these
suitable for someone who is gluten intolerant.*

CHEESY POTATO & BACON BITES

These delicious cheesy bites are made with potato gems to save time – and they add a soft, fluffy texture to the mixture.

MAKES 12 **PREP** 15 mins **COOK** 30 mins

3 eggs
2 tbs sour cream, plus extra,
   to serve
1 tbs chopped fresh chives,
   plus extra, to serve
72 (760g) frozen potato gems
2 tsp extra virgin olive oil
3 middle bacon rashers,
   finely chopped
100g (1 cup) grated pizza cheese
Sweet chilli sauce, to serve

1 Whisk the eggs, sour cream and chives in a jug until well combined. Season.

2 Preheat a pie maker. Arrange 6 potato gems in each hole. Close the lid. Cook for 10 minutes or until tender and just golden.

3 Meanwhile, heat the oil in a medium frying pan over medium-high heat. Cook the bacon, stirring occasionally, until browned. Remove from heat.

4 Sprinkle about 2 teaspoons of bacon around potato gems in each hole. Top each with 1 tablespoon of the egg mixture, then 1 tablespoon of cheese. Close the lid. Cook for 1-2 minutes until golden and just set. Transfer to a plate. Repeat assembly with potato gems, bacon, egg and cheese to make 12 bites in total.

5 Serve bites with extra sour cream, sweet chilli sauce and sprinkled with extra chives.

COOK'S TIP

For extra bite, add a sprinkling of hot paprika when you top with the cheese.

NUTRITION (EACH)

CALS	FAT	SAT FAT	PROTEIN	CARBS
215	14g	5g	8g	13g

○ FREEZABLE ● KID FRIENDLY ○ MAKE AHEAD ○ SPEEDY ○ VEGO

★★★★★

Try and stop at just eating one of these.
Kids will love them too.

RONSAUSGE

APPLE CUSTARD TEACAKES

Not so old-fashioned, now you can whip up these afternoon tea delights in a pie maker for single-serve enjoyment.

MAKES 8 **PREP** 15 mins **COOK** 20 mins

150g (1 cup) self-raising flour
100g (½ cup) caster sugar
125ml (½ cup) thick vanilla custard
2 eggs
80g butter, melted, cooled,
    plus extra, to brush
2 red apples, quartered, core
    removed, thinly sliced
Cinnamon sugar, to sprinkle

1 Sift the flour into a bowl. Stir in the sugar and make a well in the centre. Whisk the custard and eggs in a jug and pour into the well, along with the melted butter. Use a large metal spoon to fold until just combined.

2 Cut four 10cm squares of baking paper. Preheat a pie maker and lightly grease each hole. Pour ¼ cup of the custard mixture into each hole. Top with 4-5 slices of apple then cover each loosely with a square of baking paper. Close the lid. Cook for 10 minutes or until a skewer inserted in the centre of the cakes comes out clean.

3 Carefully lift out the cakes and transfer to a wire rack. Repeat using the remaining batter and apple to make 8 cakes in total.

4 While still warm, brush each cake with the extra melted butter and sprinkle with cinnamon sugar. Serve.

COOK'S TIP

Try sliced pear or peach in place of the apple.

NUTRITION (EACH)

CALS	FAT	SAT FAT	PROTEIN	CARBS
276	13g	8g	4.4g	35g

○ FREEZABLE ○ KID FRIENDLY ○ MAKE AHEAD ○ SPEEDY ● VEGO

★★★★★ *I made these GF by replacing the flour and they were a massive hit – definitely a new favourite, super easy to make and delicious.* **TANS**

NEAPOLITAN CAKES

Using only a handful of ingredients, these cute butter cakes are inspired by everyone's favourite triple-treat ice-cream.

MAKES 12 **PREP** 15 mins **COOK** 25 mins

180g butter, chopped, at room
   temperature
155g (¾ cup) caster sugar
3 eggs
225g (1½ cups) self-raising flour
80ml (⅓ cup) milk
1 tbs cocoa powder
3 drops red food colouring

1 Use electric beaters to beat the butter and sugar in a bowl until pale and creamy. Add the eggs, 1 at a time, beating well after each addition. Sift in the flour and gently fold until the mixture is just combined. Add 60ml (¼ cup) milk and fold to combine. Divide mixture evenly among 3 small bowls.

2 Add the cocoa powder and remaining milk to 1 bowl of batter and fold until combined. Add the food colouring to another bowl and fold until evenly coloured.

3 Preheat a pie maker then turn it off. Place 1 tablespoon of chocolate cake batter in each hole. Repeat with plain cake batter and pink cake batter. Close the lid and turn on the pie maker. Cook for 8 minutes or until the cakes spring back when lightly touched in the centre.

4 Transfer the cakes to a wire rack to cool. Repeat in 2 more batches, turning the pie maker off while you spoon in the batter, to make 12 cakes in total. Serve.

COOK'S TIP

Add a splash of vanilla essence to the bowl of plain cake mixture and a few drops of strawberry flavouring to the pink bowl, if you prefer.

NUTRITION (EACH)

CALS	FAT	SAT FAT	PROTEIN	CARBS
247	14g	9g	4.2g	27g

● FREEZABLE   ○ KID FRIENDLY   ● MAKE AHEAD   ○ SPEEDY   ● VEGO

HEALTHY HACK
*Use gluten-free self-raising flour for
a gluten-free version of this recipe.*

FERRERO ROCHER BOMBS

Using a cupcake packet mix, these muffins are stuffed with whole choc-hazelnut balls for the ultimate easy-yet-indulgent dessert.

MAKES 8 **PREP** 15 mins **COOK** 20 mins

100g dark chocolate melts

2 tbs thickened cream

450g packet chocolate cupcake mix (see tip)

8 Ferrero Rocher chocolate balls, unwrapped

30g (¼ cup) hazelnuts, toasted, finely chopped

Double cream or vanilla ice-cream, to serve (optional)

1 Place the chocolate melts and cream in a small heatproof bowl over a saucepan of simmering water (make sure the bowl doesn't touch the water). Cook, stirring occasionally, until the mixture is smooth. Set aside until thickened slightly.

2 Meanwhile, prepare the cupcake mixture following the packet directions (do not bake).

3 Place 2 tablespoonfuls of cupcake mixture in each hole of a pie maker. Place a chocolate ball in the centre of each. Cover with 1 tablespoon of cupcake mixture. Turn on the pie maker. Close the lid. Cook for 8 minutes or until the cakes spring back when lightly touched. Transfer to a plate and cover with a tea towel to keep warm. Repeat with remaining mixture and chocolate balls.

4 Drizzle the melted chocolate mixture over the bombs and sprinkle with hazelnuts. Serve warm with the cream or ice-cream, if using.

COOK'S TIP

To prepare the cupcake mixture, you will need the ingredients stated on the packet (ingredients may vary between brands).

NUTRITION (EACH)

CALS	FAT	SAT FAT	PROTEIN	CARBS
459	30g	15g	8g	39g

○ FREEZABLE ○ KID FRIENDLY ○ MAKE AHEAD ○ SPEEDY ● VEGO

SWAP IT OUT

*Other chocolate balls will work well with this recipe
– consider using Lindt balls too. The salted caramel
or coffee varieties would make a fun twist.*

RASPBERRY & NUTELLA
SCROLLS

It's never been faster and easier to make sweet scrolls than in a pie maker. Once you've mastered the dough, change up the fillings as much as you like.

MAKES 8 **PREP** 15 mins **COOK** 20 mins

200g (1⅓ cups) self-raising flour, plus extra, to dust
1 tbs custard powder
1 tbs icing sugar, plus extra, to dust
30g butter, chilled, chopped
125ml (½ cup) milk
160g (½ cup) Nutella
140g (1 cup) frozen raspberries, thawed

1 Sift the flour, custard powder and icing sugar into a bowl. Add the butter and use your fingertips to rub until evenly combined. Pour in the milk. Use a flat-bladed knife to mix until a sticky dough forms.

2 Gather the dough together and turn it onto a lightly floured sheet of baking paper. Gently shape into a rectangle. Dust a rolling pin with extra flour and roll dough to form a 21 x 27cm rectangle. Use fingers to shape corners and edges to make it neat.

3 Spread the dough with Nutella, leaving a 2cm gap along 1 long edge. Top evenly with raspberries. Starting from the spread-covered long side, and using the paper to help, roll into a log, finishing with the edge underneath. Use a serrated knife to cut the log into 8 even pieces.

4 Preheat a pie maker. Place a round of baking paper in the base of each pie maker hole and top with a dough scroll. Place a round of baking paper on top. Close the lid and cook for 8 minutes. Transfer scrolls to a wire rack. Repeat with remaining scrolls.

5 Serve warm or at room temperature, lightly dusted with extra icing sugar.

NUTRITION (PER SERVE)

CALS	FAT	SAT FAT	PROTEIN	CARBS
256	10g	4.4g	5g	35g

○ FREEZABLE ○ KID FRIENDLY ● MAKE AHEAD ○ SPEEDY ● VEGO

CHEESY CORN

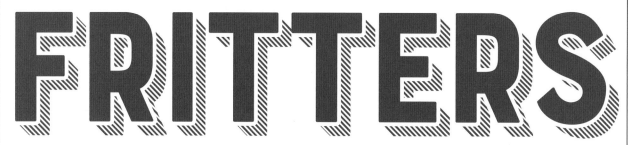

FRITTERS

Use your pie maker to whip up a batch of vegie fritters
for breakfast, lunch or an any-time-of-day snack.

MAKES 12 **PREP** 10 mins **COOK** 30 mins

2 x 420g cans corn kernels,
   rinsed, drained
100g feta, crumbled
55g (1 cup) finely grated cheddar
2 tbs chopped fresh chives,
   plus extra, to serve
75g (½ cup) self-raising flour
Pinch of cayenne pepper (optional)
2 eggs
80ml (⅓ cup) milk
Sour cream and sweet chilli sauce,
   to serve

1 Place the corn, feta, cheddar and chives in a large bowl.
Use your hands to mix until well combined. Add the flour
and cayenne, if using. Season with salt and mix until well
combined. Make a well in the centre.

2 Whisk the eggs and milk in a jug. Pour into the well and
fold until just combined (do not overmix).

3 Preheat a pie maker and lightly grease the holes with oil.
Place a ¼ cup mixture in each hole. Close the lid. Cook
for 10 minutes or until cooked through (tops will still be pale).

4 Transfer fritters to a wire rack. Repeat with the remaining
mixture in 2 more batches.

5 Season and serve warm or at room temperature, topped
with sour cream and sweet chilli sauce, and sprinkled
with extra chives.

COOK'S TIP

Add some
chopped ham
or chopped
cooked bacon to
the fritter mixture,
if you like.

NUTRITION (EACH)

CALS	FAT	SAT FAT	PROTEIN	CARBS
441	19.9g	11.6g	17.3g	46.1g

○ FREEZABLE ● KID FRIENDLY ● MAKE AHEAD ○ SPEEDY ● VEGO

10
minutes
prep

SWAP IT OUT
Substitute gluten-free self-raising flour
if you are gluten intolerant.

FLUFFY BERRY
PANCAKES

Breakfast time is easy when you use the pie maker to produce these puffy, fruit-packed pancakes. Even the kids can help!

MAKES 12 **PREP** 10 mins **COOK** 25 mins

200g (1⅓ cups) self-raising flour

2 tbs caster sugar

3 eggs

180ml (¾ cup) milk

1 tsp vanilla extract

40g butter, melted, cooled, plus extra, to grease and serve

240g fresh or thawed frozen mixed berries, plus extra fresh berries, to serve (optional)

Maple syrup, to serve

1 Sift the flour into a bowl. Stir in the sugar and make a well. Whisk the eggs, milk and vanilla in a jug. Pour into well with the melted butter. Stir until just combined (do not over mix).

2 Preheat a pie maker. Lightly brush the pie maker holes with extra butter. Place 2 level tablespoonfuls of mixture in each hole then divide one-third of the berries among the holes. Top with another level tablespoonful of mixture in each hole (it won't completely cover the berries). Close the lid. Cook for 7 minutes or until pancakes are golden brown and cooked through.

3 Transfer pancakes to a warm plate. Cover with foil to keep warm. Repeat with remaining mixture and berries in 2 more batches.

4 Serve pancakes warm with maple syrup, extra butter and extra berries, if using.

COOK'S TIP

To make assembling easier, divide the berries into 12 equal piles before you start.

NUTRITION (EACH)

CALS	FAT	SAT FAT	PROTEIN	CARBS
167	7g	4.2g	4.1g	21g

○ FREEZABLE ● KID FRIENDLY ○ MAKE AHEAD ○ SPEEDY ● VEGO

10
minutes
prep

53

LEMON SQUASH

SCONES

With just four ingredients and your trusty pie maker, you can whip up the fluffiest lemonade scones you'll ever try.

MAKES 12 **PREP** 10 mins **COOK** 25 mins

450g (3 cups) self-raising flour
300ml thickened cream
200ml lemon squash or lemonade soft drink
20g butter, melted
Double cream, to serve
Lemon curd, to serve (optional)

1 Sift the flour into a bowl and make a well. Pour cream into the well then pour in the soft drink. Use a flat-bladed knife to stir until just combined.

2 Preheat a pie maker. Place ⅓ cup of mixture in each pie maker hole. Use a pastry brush to dab a little butter on top. Close the lid. Cook for 8 minutes or until golden.

3 Transfer scones to a wire rack to cool slightly. Repeat with the remaining mixture in 2 more batches.

4 Cut the scones in half horizontally. Serve with double cream and lemon curd, if using.

COOK'S TIP

These scones are best served within 1 hour of making. Cover with a clean tea towel until ready to serve.

NUTRITION (EACH)

CALS	FAT	SAT FAT	PROTEIN	CARBS
284	16g	10g	4.7g	30g

○ FREEZABLE ● KID FRIENDLY ○ MAKE AHEAD ○ SPEEDY ● VEGO

★★★★★ *Saw this recipe and just had to make it — in the middle of the night, I might add! Absolutely fabulous and so easy.* **CHRISSY952**

10 minutes prep

HAM & FRENCH ONION TOASTIES

We've taken the humble ham and cheese toastie and given it a gourmet twist with caramelised onion and Dijon mustard.

MAKES 8 **PREP** 10 mins **COOK** 10 mins

16 slices white bread
30g butter, melted
1 tsp Dijon mustard
50g vintage cheddar, coarsely grated
60g thinly sliced ham
1 tbs caramelised onion relish, plus extra, to serve
1 tsp fresh thyme leaves, plus extra, to serve

1 Use a pie maker pastry cutter to cut 16 discs from each slice of bread. Brush 1 side of discs with melted butter. Spread 8 discs on the unbuttered side with mustard.

2 Top mustard side with half the cheese, half the ham, then the relish and thyme. Top with remaining ham and cheese. Top with remaining bread discs, buttered-side up.

3 Preheat a pie maker. Carefully place 4 sandwiches in the pie maker holes. Close the lid. Cook for 5 minutes or until golden brown. Transfer toasties to a wire rack. Repeat with remaining stacks in 1 more batch.

4 Set toasties aside to cool slightly (the filling will be very hot) before serving with extra relish and extra thyme.

COOK'S TIP

Try a good-quality tomato chutney instead of caramelised onion relish for a flavour variation.

NUTRITION (EACH)

CALS	FAT	SAT FAT	PROTEIN	CARBS
195	8g	3.9g	8g	22g

○ FREEZABLE ○ KID FRIENDLY ○ MAKE AHEAD ● SPEEDY ○ VEGO

APPLE & CUSTARD
DOUGHNUTS

Use canned apple slices from the supermarket to save time and make delicious desserts in a jiffy.

MAKES 16 **PREP** 20 mins (+15 mins chilling) **COOK** 40 mins

150g (1 cup) self-raising flour
155g (¾ cup) caster sugar
2 eggs
185ml (¾ cup) milk
1 tsp vanilla extract
90g butter, melted, cooled,
    plus extra 60g, melted
180g (⅔ cup) canned apple
    slices pie fruit
½ tsp ground cinnamon

CUSTARD
1 tbs custard powder
125ml (½ cup) milk
1 tbs caster sugar

1. For the custard, place the custard powder in a small saucepan. Add 3 teaspoons of milk and stir until smooth. Add sugar and remaining milk. Place the pan over medium-low heat and cook, stirring, for 1 minute or until the mixture boils and thickens. Transfer to a heatproof bowl and set aside, stirring occasionally, for 5 minutes or until cooled slightly. Place in the fridge for 15 minutes or until set.

2. Meanwhile, sift the flour into a large bowl. Stir in 55g (¼ cup) sugar and make a well. Whisk the eggs, milk and vanilla in a large jug and pour into the well along with the butter. Stir until just combined.

3. Preheat a pie maker. Working quickly, spoon 1 tablespoonful of batter into each pie maker hole. Top with 1 heaped teaspoonful each of the custard and apple. Cover with another tablespoonful of batter. Close the lid. Cook for 9 minutes or until the doughnuts spring back when lightly touched (they will be pale on top).

4. Transfer doughnuts to a wire rack. Repeat with the remaining batter, custard and apple in 3 more batches.

5. Combine the cinnamon and remaining sugar in a bowl. While doughnuts are still warm, use a pastry brush to brush the tops with extra melted butter. Sprinkle with the cinnamon sugar. Serve warm.

NUTRITION (EACH)

CALS	FAT	SAT FAT	PROTEIN	CARBS
172	9g	6g	2.6g	21g

○ FREEZABLE ● KID FRIENDLY ○ MAKE AHEAD ○ SPEEDY ● VEGO

CONDENSED MILK
MUFFINS

Our all-purpose muffin batter can be easily zhooshed up with your favourite flavour options, but you can keep them plain if you prefer.

MAKES 8 **PREP** 10 mins (+ cooling) **COOK** 25 mins

395g can sweetened condensed milk
125g unsalted butter, chopped
80ml (⅓ cup) milk
300g (2 cups) plain flour
2 tsp baking powder
2 eggs, lightly whisked

OPTIONAL FLAVOURS (CHOOSE 1 PER BATCH)
180g (1 cup) choc chips
120g (½ cup) hundreds and thousands
1 finely sliced red apple
125g (1 cup) fresh or frozen raspberries

1 Place condensed milk, butter and milk in a microwave-safe bowl. Microwave for 2 minutes or until melted. Stir until well combined. Set aside to cool slightly.

2 Sift the flour and baking powder into a large bowl. Make a well. Pour the egg and condensed milk mixture into the well. Stir to combine. Stir in the choc chips or hundreds and thousands, if using.

3 Preheat a pie maker. Lightly grease the pie maker holes. Divide half the mixture among prepared holes. Arrange the apple slices or berries on top, if using. Close the lid and cook for 8-10 minutes or until golden and cooked through.

4 Transfer the muffins to a wire rack. Repeat with the remaining mixture and flavour option. Serve warm or at room temperature.

COOK'S TIP

Mix and match the flavours to please everyone. You can replace the raspberries with blueberries or chopped strawberries. Or use a combo of berries, if you like.

NUTRITION (PER PLAIN MUFFIN)

CALS	FAT	SAT FAT	PROTEIN	CARBS
431	19g	12g	10g	56g

○ FREEZABLE ● KID FRIENDLY ● MAKE AHEAD ○ SPEEDY ● VEGO

★★★★★

They turned out fabulous. I used 1 cup of chopped strawberries. I'll definitely make this again.

MARGARET

VEGIE KORMA CURRY PIES

Serve these delicious vegie pies with a dollop of minted yoghurt for a real Indian-style taste sensation.

MAKES 8 **PREP** 20 mins (+ cooling) **COOK** 40 mins

2 tsp vegetable oil
1 small onion, finely chopped
2 tbs korma curry paste
400g potatoes, peeled, cut into 7mm pieces
1 carrot, peeled, chopped into 7mm pieces
125g cherry tomatoes, chopped
180ml (¾ cup) vegetable stock
60ml (¼ cup) coconut cream
80g (½ cup) frozen peas
2 sheets frozen shortcrust pastry, just thawed
2 sheets frozen puff pastry, just thawed
1 egg, lightly whisked
260g (1 cup) natural yoghurt
⅓ cup fresh mint leaves, plus extra, to serve

1 Heat the oil in a large, deep frying pan over medium heat. Add the onion and cook for 3 minutes or until softened. Stir in the curry paste and cook for 1 minute. Add the potato, carrot, tomato and stock. Stir to combine. Cover and bring to a simmer. Cook, stirring occasionally, for 10 minutes or until the vegetables are just tender.

2 Stir in the coconut cream and peas. Return to a simmer, uncovered. Cook for 5 minutes or until the liquid has reduced to a thick coating on the vegetables. Season, then set aside to cool.

3 Use pie maker pastry cutters to cut 8 large discs from shortcrust pastry and 8 small discs from puff pastry. Use a small decorative pastry cutter or knife to cut 8 shapes from the pastry scraps to decorate the tops, if you like.

4 Lightly grease holes of a pie maker. Press a shortcrust disc into each prepared hole. Place ⅓ cup of curry mixture into each pastry case. Brush 4 puff discs with egg. Decorate with pastry shapes, if using, and brush again with egg. Place puff discs on top of the filling.

5 Turn on the pie maker and close the lid. Cook for 8-10 minutes until the pastry is golden and the filling is heated through. Turn off the pie maker.

6 Lift out pies and transfer to a wire rack. Let the pie maker cool slightly then repeat with remaining pastry and curry mixture.

7 Meanwhile, place yoghurt and mint in a food processor. Process until smooth. Season the pies and sprinkle with extra mint leaves. Serve with minted yoghurt.

NUTRITION (EACH)

CALS	FAT	SAT FAT	PROTEIN	CARBS
458	26g	13g	11g	43g

○ FREEZABLE ○ KID FRIENDLY ● MAKE AHEAD ○ SPEEDY ● VEGO

HEALTHY HACK
Switch the pastry with reduced-fat shortcrust and
reduced-fat puff pastry to lower overall fat content of this dish.

CHOC-HAZELNUT FILLED
DOUGHNUTS

Add a decadent dollop of Nutella to these doughnuts for a gooey surprise in the centre.

MAKES 10 **PREP** 10 mins **COOK** 30 mins

225g (1½ cups) plain flour
2 tsp baking powder
140g (⅔ cup) caster sugar,
  plus extra 100g (½ cup)
125g butter, melted, cooled,
  plus extra 50g, melted
125g (½ cup) sour cream
2 eggs, lightly whisked
75g (¼ cup) Nutella
1 tsp ground cinnamon

1 Sift the flour and baking powder into a bowl. Stir in the sugar. Make a well. Add the butter, sour cream and egg to the well. Gently fold until combined.

2 Preheat a pie maker. Working quickly, spoon in enough batter to come two-thirds of the way up the side of each pie maker hole. Add 1 heaped teaspoon of Nutella to the centre of each and spoon over enough batter to just cover. Close the lid. Cook for 10 minutes or until golden and cooked through.

3 Meanwhile, combine the cinnamon and extra sugar in a shallow bowl. Set aside.

4 Lift out the doughnuts and transfer to a wire rack. Cover with a tea towel to keep warm. Repeat with the remaining mixture and Nutella in 2 more batches.

5 While doughnuts are still warm, use a pastry brush to brush all over with the extra butter then toss in the cinnamon sugar until completely coated. Serve warm or at room temperature.

COOK'S TIP

If you prefer jam doughnuts, replace the Nutella with your favourite jam or even lemon curd.

NUTRITION (EACH)

CALS	FAT	SAT FAT	PROTEIN	CARBS
395	22g	13g	4.4g	45g

○ FREEZABLE ● KID FRIENDLY ○ MAKE AHEAD ○ SPEEDY ● VEGO

★★★★★

These are quick, easy and delicious. Literally takes minutes to prepare and everyone was so impressed. **AMANDASTEER**

CHEESY TRUSS TOMATO TARTS

Just like an individual quiche, this simple recipe can easily be adapted using your favourite fillings and flavours.

MAKES 8   **PREP** 15 mins   **COOK** 30 mins

2 tsp olive oil
4 green shallots, thinly sliced
4 eggs
80ml (⅓ cup) thickened cream
2 sheets frozen shortcrust pastry, just thawed
80g (1 cup) coarsely grated cheddar
4 large cherry truss tomatoes, halved horizontally
Mixed salad leaves, to serve

1 Heat the oil in a small frying pan over medium heat. Cook the shallot for 2-3 minutes or until softened. Transfer to a plate to cool.

2 Whisk together the eggs and cream until they are well combined. Season.

3 Use a large pie maker pastry cutter to cut 8 discs from the pastry. Lightly grease the pie maker holes then press a pastry disc into each hole. Turn on the pie maker. Close the lid. Cook for 2-3 minutes or until pastry is partially cooked.

4 Divide half the shallot and half the cheddar among the pastry cases. Pour 2 tablespoons egg mixture into each. Nestle a tomato half, truss-side up or base-side down (without stem), in centre of each. Close the lid and cook for 10 minutes or until the egg mixture is set. Turn off the pie maker.

5 Lift out the tarts and transfer to a wire rack. Let the pie maker cool slightly then repeat with remaining pastry, shallot, cheddar, egg mixture and tomato.

6 Season. Serve the tarts warm or at room temperature with mixed salad leaves.

COOK'S TIP

Use this recipe as a base for quiche-style tarts. Replace the tomatoes with chopped ham, cooked bacon, canned salmon, cooked mushrooms or spinach.

NUTRITION (EACH)

CALS	FAT	SAT FAT	PROTEIN	CARBS
248	22g	13g	6g	18g

○ FREEZABLE   ● KID FRIENDLY   ● MAKE AHEAD   ○ SPEEDY   ● VEGO

15
minutes prep

SECRET HACK
Perfect for a cocktail party;
champagne would match well!

67

EASY BREAKFAST
FRITTATAS

Use a pie maker to create these mini breakfast treats packed with good-for-you vegies such as mushrooms and spinach.

MAKES 8 **PREP** 10 mins **COOK** 15 mins

2 tsp olive oil

3 rindless short cut bacon rashers, chopped

60g button mushrooms, halved, sliced

30g (½ cup) finely grated cheddar

20g baby spinach, shredded, plus extra leaves, to serve

5 eggs

60ml (¼ cup) thickened cream

4 cherry tomatoes, halved horizontally

Toast, to serve

1 Heat the oil in a small frying pan over medium heat. Cook the bacon for 3 minutes or until lightly browned. Transfer to a bowl. Add the mushroom to the pan and cook for 2 minutes or until softened. Transfer to the bowl with the bacon and set aside to cool slightly.

2 Preheat a pie maker. Add the cheddar and spinach to the bacon mixture and set aside. Whisk the eggs and cream in a jug. Season well.

3 Turn off the pie maker and lightly grease the holes. Divide half the bacon mixture among the prepared holes. Pour half the egg mixture over the top. Place a cherry tomato half, cut-side up, in the centres. Close the lid and turn on the pie maker. Cook for 5 minutes or until set and golden brown.

4 Lift out the frittatas and transfer to a plate. Repeat with the remaining bacon and egg mixtures. Serve with toast and extra spinach.

COOK'S TIP

These frittatas make great picnic food and are just as tasty served at room temperature.

NUTRITION (EACH)

CALS	FAT	SAT FAT	PROTEIN	CARBS
211	10g	3.9g	13g	17g

○ FREEZABLE ● KID FRIENDLY ● MAKE AHEAD ● SPEEDY ○ VEGO

BLACK BEAN QUESADILLAS

These vegetarian quesadillas are a great low-cal snack for hungry teens. They'll disappear quickly!

MAKES 12 **PREP** 10 mins **COOK** 15 mins

6 x 22cm flour tortillas
400g can black beans, rinsed, drained
85g (⅓ cup) bought tomato salsa
120g finely grated cheddar
Fresh tomato salsa, to serve (see tip)
Chopped fresh coriander leaves, sour cream and lime wedges, to serve

1 Use 9cm and 8cm pastry cutters or a small sharp knife (and small bowls as a guide) to cut two 9cm discs and two 8cm discs from each tortilla to make 24 discs in total. Spray 1 side of each disc with oil. Cover with plastic wrap to prevent drying out. Combine the beans and bought salsa in a bowl.

2 Preheat a pie maker. Place a 9cm tortilla disc, oil-side down, in each pie maker hole. Place a slightly heaped tablespoonful of mixture in each tortilla case. Top with 1 tablespoon cheddar. Place an 8cm tortilla disc, oil-side up, on top of each. Close the lid. Cook for 5 minutes or until the quesadillas are golden and the filling is warmed through.

3 Transfer quesadillas to a wire rack. Repeat with the remaining tortilla discs and mixture in 2 more batches.

4 Top the quesadillas with fresh salsa and scatter with coriander. Serve with sour cream and lime wedges.

COOK'S TIP

Make a quick fresh salsa with chopped cherry tomatoes, thinly sliced green shallots and a squeeze of lime juice.

NUTRITION (EACH)

CALS	FAT	SAT FAT	PROTEIN	CARBS
179	11g	5.4g	6g	14g

○ FREEZABLE   ● KID FRIENDLY   ○ MAKE AHEAD   ● SPEEDY   ● VEGO

10
minutes
prep

FOUR-INGREDIENT BANANA MUFFINS

One pie maker plus four ingredients equals eight muffins: lunch-box fillers don't get easier than this.

MAKES 8 **PREP** 10 mins **COOK** 20 mins

2 overripe bananas, plus extra
  1 ripe banana (see tips)
125g (½ cup) whole egg mayonnaise
60g (¼ cup) caster sugar
150g (1 cup) self-raising flour
Butter and/or honey, to serve
  (optional)

1 Preheat a pie maker. Peel overripe bananas and transfer to a bowl. Use a fork to mash. Add the mayonnaise, sugar and 2 tablespoons water. Whisk with fork until well combined. Peel the extra ripe banana and chop into 8 even pieces.

2 Sift the flour over the banana mixture. Use a metal spoon to gently fold until combined. Drop ¼ cup of mixture into each pie maker hole. Top each with a piece of ripe banana in the centre. Close the lid and cook for 8 minutes.

3 Transfer muffins to a wire rack. Repeat with remaining mixture and banana pieces.

4 Serve the muffins warm or at room temperature with butter to spread and/or honey to drizzle, if using.

COOK'S TIPS

The riper the bananas, the sweeter and more flavoursome they are for cooking. Don't worry if the skin is almost black!
Opt for a good-quality mayonnaise that has a more neutral flavour.

NUTRITION (EACH)

CALS	FAT	SAT FAT	PROTEIN	CARBS
238	12g	1.6g	2.5g	29g

★★★★★ *Easy peasy. So easy, so tasty, no refusals from the kids.* **JUSTINE FERGUSON**

● FREEZABLE ● KID FRIENDLY ● MAKE AHEAD ● SPEEDY ● VEGO

MINI IMPOSSIBLE QUICHES

These tasty little snacks, called 'impossible' because they bake their own crust, are perfect for lunch boxes or as after-school tummy fillers.

MAKES 12 **PREP** 10 mins **COOK** 30 mins

150g (1 cup) plain flour
3 eggs
250ml (1 cup) milk
125ml (½ cup) thickened cream
100g smoked ham, chopped
80g grated cheddar, coarsely grated, plus extra 100g, cut into 12 pieces
2 green shallots, thinly sliced, plus extra, thinly sliced, to serve

1 Sift the flour into a bowl. Make a well and add the eggs. Whisk until smooth. Slowly whisk in the milk and cream until smooth. Season. Stir in the ham, cheddar and shallot. Transfer mixture to a large jug.

2 Preheat a pie maker. Pour in enough mixture to fill each pie maker hole. Close the lid. Cook for 4 minutes. Place a piece of extra cheddar in the centre of each quiche. Cook for 4-5 minutes until cooked through and golden.

3 Transfer quiches to a plate. Cover with a tea towel to keep warm. Repeat with remaining mixture and cheddar in 2 more batches (see tip).

4 To serve quiches warm or at room temperature, season and scatter with extra shallot.

COOK'S TIP

Stir the egg mixture well between each batch. This will prevent the flour from sinking to the bottom of the mixture.

NUTRITION (EACH)

CALS	FAT	SAT FAT	PROTEIN	CARBS
186	12g	7g	9g	11g

★★★★★ *This is my first recipe using my pie maker and I will definitely be using it again. I added some frozen peas and corn.* **KKP21**

○ FREEZABLE ● KID FRIENDLY ● MAKE AHEAD ○ SPEEDY ○ VEGO

10
minutes
prep

FOUR-CHEESE CALZONES

These mini calzones with tomato, ham and basil make great party food (or a stellar weeknight dinner).

MAKES 8   **PREP** 10 mins   **COOK** 10 mins

16 slices wholemeal bread
80ml (⅓ cup) tomato pasta sauce
80g sliced ham or salami
125g (½ cup) fresh ricotta
80g (½ cup) grated 3-cheese blend
16 small fresh basil leaves, plus
   extra, to serve

1 Use a pie maker pastry cutter to cut 16 large discs from the bread.

2 Press 1 bread disc into each hole of the pie maker. Spread each bread case with ½ tablespoon pasta sauce. Divide half the ham or salami among the cases and top each with 1 tablespoon ricotta and 1 tablespoon cheese blend. Top each with 2 basil leaves and 1 of the remaining bread discs. Spray with oil.

3 Turn on the pie maker and close the lid. Cook for 5 minutes or until the filling is warmed through and the bread is golden. Turn off the pie maker.

4 Lift out the calzones and transfer to a wire rack. Repeat with remaining bread and filling.

5 Sprinkle the calzones with extra basil and serve immediately.

COOK'S TIP

Try mushrooms instead of ham or salami, or even shredded cooked chicken in the filling.

NUTRITION (EACH)

CALS	FAT	SAT FAT	PROTEIN	CARBS
211	7g	3.7g	12g	23g

○ FREEZABLE   ● KID FRIENDLY   ○ MAKE AHEAD   ● SPEEDY   ○ VEGO

SPINACH & THREE-CHEESE PIES

The whole family will love these super-easy filo pies.
Make ahead and freeze for school or work.

MAKES 16 **PREP** 30 mins (+ 15 mins chilling) **COOK** 1 hour 15 mins

1 tbs extra virgin olive oil
1 brown onion, finely chopped
1 bunch English spinach, leaves
    roughly chopped
1 green shallot, finely chopped
¼ cup finely chopped fresh
    mint leaves
150g feta, crumbled
150g fresh ricotta, crumbled
40g (½ cup) finely grated parmesan
2 eggs
10 sheets filo pastry
80g butter, melted

1 Heat the oil in a large frying pan over medium-high heat. Add the onion. Cook, stirring, for 5 minutes or until softened. Add the spinach, shallot and mint. Cook, stirring, for 3 minutes or until wilted and all liquid is evaporated. Transfer to a large bowl and place in the fridge for 15 minutes to chill.

2 Add the feta, ricotta, parmesan and eggs to cooled spinach mixture. Season with pepper. Stir until well combined.

3 Place 1 filo sheet on a clean surface. Brush with butter. Top with another filo sheet and butter. Repeat using 3 more sheets of filo, finishing with butter. Repeat layering to make a second stack. Cut each stack in half lengthways. Cut each half crossways into 12 even strips (48 strips).

4 Preheat a pie maker. Brush 3 filo strips with butter then criss-cross in a star pattern. Repeat to make 3 more filo stars. Press a star into each pie maker hole (pastry will extend out of holes). Quickly place 2 level tablespoonfuls of spinach mixture into each pastry case. Fold over excess pastry to partially cover filling. Brush with a little more butter. Close the lid. Cook for 16 minutes or until golden.

5 Transfer pies to a wire rack. Repeat with remaining filo strips, spinach mixture and butter in 3 more batches. Serve warm or at room temperature.

NUTRITION (EACH)

CALS	FAT	SAT FAT	PROTEIN	CARBS
146	10g	5.8g	6.5g	6g

● FREEZABLE ● KID FRIENDLY ● MAKE AHEAD ○ SPEEDY ● VEGO

★★★★★

I was worried the spinach wouldn't go down well with miss 5, but she loved them. Going to start putting them in her lunch box.

NATALIEMULLAN

30 minutes prep

SPINACH & FETA GOZLEME

Make your favourite street-food snack at home in your pie maker,
with the same delicious spinach and feta filling and flaky pastry.

MAKES 10 **PREP** 20 mins **COOK** 30 mins

250g pkt frozen spinach, thawed,
  excess liquid drained
100g feta, crumbled
100g (1 cup) coarsely grated
  mozzarella
1 green shallot, thinly sliced
2 tbs finely chopped fresh
  mint leaves
9 sheets filo pastry
70g butter, melted
Sesame seeds, to decorate
  (optional)
Greek-style yoghurt and lemon
  wedges, to serve

1 Combine the spinach, feta, mozzarella, shallot and mint in a large bowl and mix until evenly combined.

2 Place 1 sheet of filo on a clean surface. Brush with butter. Top with another filo sheet and butter. Repeat using 4 more sheets, finishing with butter. Cut in half lengthways then each into thirds crossways to make 6 filo stacks.

3 Place a filo stack in each hole of the pie maker, allowing the filo to overhang the side. Fill each case with spinach filling. Fold overhanging pastry over the filling. Brush with butter. Turn on the pie maker and close the lid. Cook for 5 minutes. Turn over and cook for a further 5 minutes, sprinkling with sesame seeds in the last minute of cooking, if using. Lift out the gozleme and transfer to a plate. Cover with foil to keep warm.

4 Meanwhile, place 1 remaining filo sheet on a clean surface and brush with butter. Repeat layering with the remaining filo sheets and butter. Fold in half then cut into 4 filo stacks.

5 Repeat cooking with the remaining filo stacks, filling and sesame seeds to make 10 gozleme. Serve with yoghurt and lemon wedges.

NUTRITION (EACH)

CALS	FAT	SAT FAT	PROTEIN	CARBS
172	12g	7g	7g	9g

○ FREEZABLE ○ KID FRIENDLY ○ MAKE AHEAD ○ SPEEDY ● VEGO

★★★★★
Very tasty and easy! I didn't brush with butter, I used olive oil spray – same result.
BRENDA TUCKER

20 minutes prep

FRITTATAS WITH INSTANT NOODLES

Turn instant noodles into individual frittatas using your pie maker.
The whole family will love these savoury snacks.

MAKES 12 **PREP** 10 mins (+15 mins cooling) **COOK** 35 mins

2 x 72g pkt chicken-flavoured
   instant noodles
6 eggs
1 large carrot, peeled,
   coarsely grated
1 green shallot, thinly sliced
230g (1½ cups) frozen peas,
   corn and capsicum
65g (¾ cup) coarsely grated cheddar

1 Cook the noodles following packet directions, reserving 1 seasoning sachet (save remaining sachet for another use). Drain well. Set aside for 15 minutes to cool. Use scissors to cut the noodles into 12cm lengths.

2 Lightly whisk eggs in a large bowl. Add the noodles, carrot, shallot, frozen vegetables, cheddar and reserved seasoning sachet. Stir until well combined.

3 Preheat a pie maker. Pour ¼ cup of mixture into each pie maker hole. Close the lid. Cook for 10 minutes or until golden and set.

4 Transfer frittatas to a wire rack to cool. Repeat with remaining mixture in 2 more batches. Serve warm or at room temperature.

COOK'S TIP

These are delicious served at room temperature, so pop a couple in your work or school lunch box!

NUTRITION (EACH)

CALS	FAT	SAT FAT	PROTEIN	CARBS
97	5g	2.2g	6g	6g

○ FREEZABLE ● KID FRIENDLY ● MAKE AHEAD ○ SPEEDY ● VEGO

★★★★★
With three pretty fussy eaters this was an awesome recipe that we got to test our new pie maker out on. All three ate all of what was on their plates including the slightly hidden veg. Great option. **CHARLESMC**

10 minutes prep

CREAM CHEESE-ICED
GINGERBREAD

Using pantry ingredients, these simple gingerbread cakes with cream cheese icing are ready in no time.

MAKES 10 **PREP** 10 mins **COOK** 25 mins

225g (1½ cups) self-raising flour
155g (¾ cup) brown sugar
2 tsp ground ginger
1 tsp mixed spice
2 eggs
125ml (½ cup) milk
125g butter, melted, cooled
Ground cinnamon, to sprinkle
   (optional)

ICING
250g tub spreadable cream cheese
2 tbs icing sugar mixture
2 tsp fresh lemon juice

1 Sift the flour, sugar, ginger and mixed spice into a large bowl. Make a well. Whisk the eggs and milk in a bowl then add to the well with the butter. Use a large metal spoon to fold until just combined.

2 Turn on a pie maker. Place ¼ cup of mixture into each pie maker hole. Close the lid. Cook for 7 minutes.

3 Transfer cakes to a wire rack to cool completely. Repeat with the remaining mixture in 2 more batches to make 10 cakes in total.

4 For the icing, stir all the ingredients together in a small bowl until smooth. Spread the icing over the cakes and dust with cinnamon, if using. Serve.

COOK'S TIPS

Decorate with red and green sprinkles for a Christmas treat. These little cakes can be frozen without the icing. Thaw before icing and devouring!

NUTRITION (EACH)

CALS	FAT	SAT FAT	PROTEIN	CARBS
318	18g	12g	6g	33g

● FREEZABLE ● KID FRIENDLY ● MAKE AHEAD ○ SPEEDY ● VEGO

★★★★★
So delicious and so easy.
I'll be making these for Christmas!
SUNNYBOO

HEARTY CLASSIC
MEAT PIES

Homemade meat pies are even better than the ones you get at the footy. Try this take on an Aussie classic recipe.

MAKES 8 **PREP** 10 mins (+30 mins cooling) **COOK** 40 mins

1 tbs olive oil
1 brown onion, finely chopped
500g beef mince
50g (⅓ cup) gravy mix
60ml (¼ cup) tomato sauce,
    plus extra, to serve
1 tbs Worcestershire sauce
White pepper, to season
4 sheets frozen puff pastry,
    just thawed
1 egg, lightly whisked

1 Heat the oil in a large frying pan over medium heat. Add the onion and cook, stirring often, for 2 minutes or until softened. Add the beef and cook, stirring with a wooden spoon to break up any lumps, for 5 minutes or until browned and cooked through.

2 Sprinkle in the gravy mix. Stir to coat. Add 250ml (1 cup) water and cook, stirring, for 1 minute or until the sauce thickens slightly. Add the tomato sauce and Worcestershire sauce. Season with salt and white pepper. Simmer, stirring often, for 10 minutes or until thick. Remove from heat. Cover and set aside for 30 minutes to cool.

3 Use a pie maker pastry cutters to cut 8 large and 8 small discs from the pastry. Press a large pastry disc into each pie maker hole. Divide half the mixture among pastry cases. Top each with a small pastry disc. Brush with egg. Turn on the pie maker. Close the lid. Cook for 10 minutes or until the pastry is golden.

4 Transfer pies to a plate and cover with a tea towel to keep warm. Repeat with remaining pastry, filling and egg. Serve the pies warm with extra tomato sauce.

COOK'S TIPS

Try lamb, pork or chicken mince instead of beef, if you prefer. Just use a chicken gravy mix. Make the filling up to 3 days ahead and store in an airtight container in the fridge.

NUTRITION (EACH)

CALS	FAT	SAT FAT	PROTEIN	CARBS
433	24g	13g	20g	33g

○ FREEZABLE ● KID FRIENDLY ● MAKE AHEAD ○ SPEEDY ○ VEGO

★★★★★

*I cannot believe how easy, fun and tasty
the things you can do with a pie maker are.
I used the Taste recipe and
I don't think I will buy pies again.*

RAYLON

10 minutes prep

ZUCCHINI SLICE MUFFINS

This no-hassle version of your favourite zucchini slice treat means you don't have to warm up the oven or wash up the pan.

MAKES 10 **PREP** 10 mins **COOK** 30 mins

2 (about 300g) zucchini,
   coarsely grated
80ml (⅓ cup) extra virgin olive oil
200g sweet potato, peeled,
   coarsely grated
150g (1 cup) self-raising flour
5 eggs, lightly beaten
100g (1 cup) pre-grated
   3-cheese blend

1 Place the zucchini in a colander. Use clean hands to squeeze out excess liquid. Transfer to a large bowl.

2 Heat 1 tablespoon of oil in a non-stick frying pan over medium-high heat. Add sweet potato and cook, stirring occasionally, for 5 minutes or until softened. Add to zucchini.

3 Sift the flour into the bowl. Add the egg, cheese and remaining oil. Season and stir until well combined.

4 Preheat a pie maker. Evenly fill the holes with the zucchini mixture. Close the lid. Cook for 8 minutes or until set and golden.

5 Lift out the muffins and transfer to a wire rack. Repeat with the remaining mixture in 2 more batches. Serve the muffins warm or at room temperature.

COOK'S TIP

For an extra flavour hit, pan-fry chopped short cut bacon and add to the zucchini mixture.

NUTRITION (PER SERVE)

CALS	FAT	SAT FAT	PROTEIN	CARBS
166	10g	2.6g	5g	14g

● FREEZABLE ● KID FRIENDLY ● MAKE AHEAD ○ SPEEDY ● VEGO

CHEESY GARLIC BREAD
BOMBS

An explosion of melted mozzarella is the surprise inside these tasty morsels. Serve as a side with pasta or minestrone.

MAKES 8 **PREP** 25 mins **COOK** 25 mins

300g (2 cups) plain flour
2 tsp baking powder
80g chilled unsalted butter, finely chopped, plus extra 60g, chopped
185ml (¾ cup) milk
3 garlic cloves, crushed
⅓ cup chopped fresh basil leaves, plus extra leaves, to serve (optional)
80g mozzarella, cut into 8 pieces

1 Place the flour and baking powder in a large bowl. Add the butter. Use your fingertips to rub the butter into the flour mixture until it resembles coarse crumbs. Make a well in the centre.

2 Pour the milk into the well. Use a flat-bladed knife to stir until the dough just comes together. Turn onto a lightly floured surface. Knead briefly until dough is smooth, then divide into 8 even pieces.

3 Place the garlic and extra butter in a microwave-safe bowl. Microwave for 1 minute or until melted. Stir in the basil.

4 Roll 1 dough portion into an 8cm disc. Dip a piece of mozzarella in butter mixture then place in the centre of the dough disc. Bring 2 sides up to enclose the coated mozzarella and press together to seal. Roll into a ball (the butter will ooze out and coat the dough ball). Repeat with the remaining dough, mozzarella and butter mixture.

5 Preheat a pie maker. Place 4 bread bombs, seam-side down, in the holes. Cook for 6 minutes. Brush with some remaining butter mixture and turn over. Cook for a further 6 minutes.

6 Transfer bread bombs to a plate. Cover with foil to keep warm. Cook remaining bread bombs. Season and serve sprinkled with extra basil, if using.

NUTRITION (PER SERVE)

CALS	FAT	SAT FAT	PROTEIN	CARBS
307	18g	11g	7g	29g

○ FREEZABLE ● KID FRIENDLY ○ MAKE AHEAD ○ SPEEDY ● VEGO

PUDDINGS WITH MOLTEN
CHOCOLATE

These oozy chocolate puds are so good they won't last 30 seconds when served. Luckily, they take no time at all to make!

MAKES 6 **PREP** 5 mins **COOK** 15 mins

180g dark chocolate (70% cocoa), chopped
150g unsalted butter, chopped
110g (½ cup) caster sugar
50g (⅓ cup) plain flour
4 eggs, lightly beaten
Cocoa powder, to dust
Vanilla ice-cream and fresh raspberries, to serve

1. Place chocolate and butter in a saucepan over medium-low heat. Cook, stirring occasionally, for 2-3 minutes or until melted and combined. Remove from heat.

2. Add the sugar, flour and egg to the pan. Quickly whisk to combine (see tip).

3. Preheat a pie maker. Pour ⅓ cupful of the chocolate mixture into each pie maker hole. Close the lid. Cook for 3-4 minutes until a crust forms on the top. Transfer puddings to a wire rack.

4. Repeat with the remaining mixture to make 2 more puddings.

5. Dust puddings with cocoa and serve immediately with ice-cream and berries.

COOK'S TIP

Don't overbeat the mixture in step 2 – just whisk so that the ingredients are evenly combined.

NUTRITION (PER SERVE)

CALS	FAT	SAT FAT	PROTEIN	CARBS
577	37g	23g	9g	54g

○ FREEZABLE ● KID FRIENDLY ○ MAKE AHEAD ● SPEEDY ● VEGO

5
minutes prep

★★★★★

Loved these very much. So quick and easy and tasty.
Kids thought they were amazing!!!

THE DOVEL QUEEN

EASY INDIVIDUAL CHERRY PIES

These mini cherry pies taste just like Granny used to bake.
If only she'd had a pie maker to put them together this easily.

MAKES 8   **PREP** 15 mins (+ 1 hour chilling)   **COOK** 40 mins

1 tbs fresh lemon juice
500g pkt frozen pitted cherries
½ tsp mixed spice
75g (⅓ cup) raw sugar
2 tbs cornflour
1 tbs cold water
4 sheets frozen shortcrust pastry,
   just thawed
1 egg white, lightly whisked

1 Combine the lemon juice, cherries, mixed spice and 60g (¼ cup) sugar in a saucepan over medium heat. Cook, stirring, for 5 minutes or until the cherries thaw and sugar dissolves. Mix the cornflour and cold water in a small bowl, then stir into the cherry mixture. Increase heat to medium-high. Cook, stirring, for 2 minutes or until the mixture boils and thickens. Transfer to a large heatproof bowl. Place in the fridge for 1 hour to cool completely.

2 Preheat a pie maker. Use the pie maker pastry cutters to cut 8 large discs from 2 pastry sheets and 8 small discs from the remaining 2 pastry sheets.

3 Place a large pastry disc in each pie maker hole. Spoon ¼ cupful of cherry mixture into each pastry case. Top each with a small pastry disc. Lightly press the edges to seal. Close the lid and cook for 14 minutes.

4 Working quickly, lift the lid and brush the tops with egg white. Sprinkle with 2 teaspoons of the remaining sugar. Close the lid. Cook for a further 2 minutes or until the pies are golden.

5 Transfer pies to a wire rack to cool. Repeat with remaining pastry, cherry mixture, egg and sugar to make 8 pies. Serve warm or at room temperature.

NUTRITION (PER SERVE)

CALS	FAT	SAT FAT	PROTEIN	CARBS
407	18g	8g	6g	53g

○ FREEZABLE   ○ KID FRIENDLY   ● MAKE AHEAD   ○ SPEEDY   ● VEGO

★★★★★

*I love this recipe. I have used other berries
and they still turn out delicious and look amazing.*

TAHLI

LEMON DELICIOUS PUDDINGS

A super-quick dessert that zings on the tastebuds. These are perfect for a dinner party or mid-week indulgence.

MAKES 8 **PREP** 10 mins **COOK** 15 mins

185ml (¾ cup) milk
2 tbs fresh lemon juice
2 tsp finely grated lemon rind
150g (1 cup) self-raising flour
35g (¼ cup) custard powder
55g (¼ cup) caster sugar
2 eggs, lightly beaten
100g butter, melted, cooled
1 tbs bought lemon curd
Icing sugar, to dust

1 Place the milk, lemon juice and rind in a jug and whisk until combined.

2 Preheat a pie maker. Sift the flour and custard powder into a large bowl. Stir in the caster sugar. Make a well in the centre. Pour the milk mixture into the well then the egg and butter. Use a metal spoon to stir until just combined.

3 Place 2 tablespoons of mixture in each hole of the pie maker. Add ½ teaspoon lemon curd to the centres of each. Top with another 2 tablespoons of mixture. Close the lid. Cook for 7 minutes or until just set. Turn off the pie maker. Transfer puddings to a wire rack. Repeat with the remaining mixture and curd.

4 Serve the lemon delicious puddings immediately dusted with icing sugar.

COOK'S TIP

For a mixed citrus flavour, replace the lemon juice and rind with lime or orange.

NUTRITION (PER SERVE)

CALS	FAT	SAT FAT	PROTEIN	CARBS
245	13g	8g	4.5g	29g

★★★★★

First time giving these (and the pie maker) a whirl. Absolutely true to its name — delicious!! **ANUTTY**

○ FREEZABLE ○ KID FRIENDLY ○ MAKE AHEAD ● SPEEDY ● VEGO

BERRY APPLE STAR TARTS

Filled to the brim with fruit, and surrounded by melt-in-your-mouth shortcrust pastry, these are bound to be a star attraction!

MAKES 12 **PREP** 15 mins **COOK** 30 mins

800g can apple slices pie fruit
185g fresh or frozen raspberries
55g (¼ cup) caster sugar
¼ tsp ground cinnamon
6 sheets frozen shortcrust pastry, just thawed (see tip)
Icing sugar, to dust
Vanilla ice-cream, to serve

1 Place the apple, raspberries, sugar and cinnamon in a bowl and stir gently to combine.

2 Use pie maker pastry cutters to cut 12 large and 12 small discs from the pastry. Use a small decorative cutter to cut out a star shape in the centre of the small pastry discs.

3 Lightly grease the holes of a pie maker. Press a large pastry disc into each hole. Place ⅓ cup of the mixture in each pastry case. Place small pastry discs on top.

4 Turn on the pie maker and close the lid. Cook for 8-10 minutes or until the pastry is golden brown and the filling is cooked through. Turn off the pie maker.

5 Transfer pies to a wire rack. Let the pie maker cool slightly then repeat with the remaining pastry and mixture in 2 more batches.

6 Dust the berry apple pies with icing sugar and serve warm with ice-cream.

COOK'S TIP

Use good-quality sweet homemade shortcrust pastry, or sweet shortcrust pastry bought from specialty food stores, to take these pies to the next level.

NUTRITION (PER SERVE)

CALS	FAT	SAT FAT	PROTEIN	CARBS
245	23g	11g	6g	55g

○ FREEZABLE ● KID FRIENDLY ○ MAKE AHEAD ○ SPEEDY ● VEGO

CHOCOLATE & ZUCCHINI BITES

Yes, this combo really works! The zucchini makes these chocolatey cakes extra moist. And you'll be serving the kids vegies without them knowing.

MAKES 12 **PREP** 15 mins **COOK** 25 mins

1½ cups (about 2 large) finely grated zucchini
160g (1 cup, lightly packed) brown sugar
165ml (⅔ cup) light-flavoured olive oil
2 eggs
1 tsp vanilla bean paste
225g (1½ cups) plain flour
35g (⅓ cup) cocoa powder
1 tsp baking powder
Pure icing sugar, to dust

1 Place the zucchini in a colander and use clean hands to squeeze out excess liquid (see tip).

2 Place the sugar and oil in a large bowl. Whisk until well combined. Add the eggs and vanilla and whisk to combine. Sift in the flour, cocoa and baking powder. Stir until just combined. Add the zucchini and stir until combined.

3 Preheat a pie maker. Place ¼ cup of the mixture into each hole. Close the lid. Cook for 8 minutes or until a skewer inserted into the centres comes out clean. Turn off the pie maker. Transfer cakes to a wire rack to cool.

4 Repeat with the remaining mixture in 2 more batches. Serve the cakes dusted with icing sugar.

NUTRITION (PER SERVE)

CALS	FAT	SAT FAT	PROTEIN	CARBS
250	14g	2.4g	3.6g	27g

COOK'S TIP

The addition of zucchini makes these cakes moist. You'll need about 2 large zucchini for this recipe. Be sure to squeeze as much of the excess liquid from the grated zucchini as you can.

○ FREEZABLE ● KID FRIENDLY ● MAKE AHEAD ○ SPEEDY ● VEGO

SWAP IT OUT

*Use gluten-free flour and baking powder
to make this suitable for people who are gluten-intolerant.*

LEMON JELLY CAKES

These zesty little cakes, oozing with cream and lemon curd, will go down a treat for afternoon tea, dessert, or just because!

MAKES 8 **PREP** 40 mins (+ 1 hour setting, cooling) **COOK** 20 mins

85g pkt lemon-flavoured
   jelly crystals
250ml (1 cup) boiling water
125g unsalted butter, chopped,
   at room temperature
100g (½ cup) caster sugar
2 eggs
150g (1 cup) plain flour
1 tsp baking powder
80ml (⅓ cup) milk
170g (2 cups) desiccated coconut,
   plus extra, to serve
Bought lemon curd and whipped
   cream, to serve

1 Pour the jelly crystals into a shallow heatproof dish. Add the boiling water and stir until the crystals dissolve. Stir in 125ml (½ cup) tap water. Set aside for 1 hour or until thick but not set.

2 Meanwhile, use electric beaters to beat the butter and sugar in a bowl until pale and creamy. Add the eggs, 1 at a time, beating well after each addition.

3 Combine the flour and baking powder in a bowl then, alternating with the milk, fold into the butter mixture until combined.

4 Preheat a pie maker. Divide half the mixture among the pie maker holes. Cook for 10 minutes or until a skewer inserted into the centres comes out clean.

5 Lift out the cakes and transfer to a wire rack to cool slightly. Repeat with the remaining mixture.

6 Place the coconut on a large plate. Working in batches, place the cakes in the jelly mixture for 30 seconds to soak. Turn the cakes over and soak for a further 30 seconds. Lift out and place in the coconut. Press well, turning, to coat all over. Transfer the cakes to a plate and set aside to cool completely.

7 Use a large serrated knife to cut the cakes in half horizontally. Dollop lemon curd and whipped cream in the centre of each bottom half of the cakes. Top with the remaining cake halves. Sprinkle with extra coconut to serve.

NUTRITION (PER SERVE)

CALS	FAT	SAT FAT	PROTEIN	CARBS
510	33g	25g	7g	47g

○ FREEZABLE ○ KID FRIENDLY ○ MAKE AHEAD ○ SPEEDY ● VEGO

SWAP IT OUT

Any citrus flavour would work with this recipe — try lime or orange curd for a sweeter touch.

CONDENSED MILK RIPPLE

DESSERTS

These mini cakes are made with bought biscuits sandwiched around a rich chocolate filling. Yum!

MAKES 8 **PREP** 10 mins **COOK** 10 mins

COOK'S TIP

As you only need a small amount of condensed milk, instead of opening a can, simply use condensed milk in a tube.

4 eggs
80ml (⅓ cup) sweetened condensed milk
2 tbs cocoa powder
16 chocolate ripple biscuits
Dark chocolate and vanilla ice-cream, to serve

1 Preheat a pie maker. Whisk the eggs, condensed milk and cocoa in a large bowl until combined (don't worry if the cocoa is a little bit lumpy).

2 Place a biscuit in each hole of the pie maker hole. Drizzle 1 tablespoon of the cocoa mixture over top of each biscuit. Top with another biscuit and another tablespoonful of mixture. Close the lid and cook for 4 minutes.

3 Transfer cakes to a plate. While still warm, finely grate dark chocolate over the tops.

4 Stir the mixture then repeat cooking with the remaining biscuits and mixture. Serve cakes with ice-cream.

NUTRITION (PER SERVE)

CALS	FAT	SAT FAT	PROTEIN	CARBS
260	12g	7g	7g	31g

★★★★★

GARB67

○ FREEZABLE ● KID FRIENDLY ○ MAKE AHEAD ● SPEEDY ● VEGO

10
minutes
prep

CHEESECAKE SWIRL
BROWNIES

For something a bit special, whip up a batch of these choc-raspberry delights. They'll win hearts every time.

MAKES 16 **PREP** 15 mins **COOK** 45 mins

185g butter, chopped
300g dark chocolate, chopped
160g (1 cup, lightly packed) dark brown sugar
150g (¾ cup) caster sugar
4 eggs
225g (1½ cups) plain flour
30g (¼ cup) cocoa powder
60g (½ cup) frozen raspberries, thawed, torn

VANILLA CREAM CHEESE SWIRL
125g cream cheese, at room temperature
1 tbs caster sugar
1 egg yolk
1 tsp vanilla extract

1 Place the butter and chocolate in a saucepan over medium-low heat. Cook, stirring occasionally, for 5 minutes or until melted. Remove from heat.

2 Meanwhile, to make the cream cheese swirl, use electric beaters to beat the cream cheese and caster sugar in a bowl until smooth. Add the egg yolk and vanilla. Beat until well combined. Spoon mixture into a sealable plastic bag.

3 Whisk the brown sugar and caster sugar into the chocolate mixture until well combined. Whisk in eggs. Sift in the flour and cocoa. Stir until well combined.

4 Preheat a pie maker. Spoon ¼ cupful of chocolate mixture into each hole of the pie maker. Snip 1 corner off the sealable bag. Pipe 4 small dollops of cream cheese mixture on top of the chocolate mixture in each hole. Use a skewer to swirl both mixtures to create a marbled effect. Top each with 3 raspberry pieces.

5 Close the lid. Cook for 8 minutes. Turn off the pie maker. Keep lid closed for 2 minutes or until the brownies are just firm when lightly touched and crumbs cling to a skewer inserted into centres. Transfer brownies to a wire rack to cool.

6 Repeat with the remaining chocolate and cream cheese mixtures, and raspberries, in 3 more batches. Serve warm or at room temperature.

NUTRITION (PER SERVE)

CALS	FAT	SAT FAT	PROTEIN	CARBS
365	18.8g	11.4g	4.8g	44.4g

○ FREEZABLE ○ KID FRIENDLY ● MAKE AHEAD ○ SPEEDY ● VEGO

15
minutes
prep

★★★★★

I've made these a few times now and they are a hit every time!
So tasty, and pretty too! **NB!**

SAUSAGE ROLL MAKER

OPEN THE DOOR TO A WHOLE NEW WORLD
OF DELICIOUSNESS WITH NEW FILLINGS
FOR THIS CLASSIC FAVOURITE.

EASY HALOUMI FINGERS

Try our easy take on classic spinach and cheese triangles
– silverbeet, haloumi and mozzarella toasted snugly in mountain bread.

MAKES 8 **PREP** 15 mins **COOK** 30 mins

1 tbs extra virgin olive oil
2 garlic cloves, finely chopped
4 cups shredded fresh
  silverbeet leaves
180g pkt haloumi, coarsely grated
80g (1 cup) shredded mozzarella
2 tbs chopped fresh continental
  parsley
2 pieces mountain bread, quartered
Tzatziki, to serve
Lemon wedges, to serve
Fresh mint leaves, to serve (optional)

1 Heat oil in a large non-stick frying pan over medium-high heat. Add the garlic and cook, stirring, for 1 minute or until aromatic. Add silverbeet and cook, tossing occasionally, for 5 minutes or until just wilted. Transfer to a bowl.

2 Add the haloumi, mozzarella and parsley to the bowl. Stir to combine. Cut the bread into quarters.

3 Working quickly, arrange half of the silverbeet mixture along the bottom edges of 4 mountain bread quarters. Tuck in the sides and roll up to enclose the filling. Place, seam side down, in the sausage roll maker. Spray with oil. Close the lid and turn on. Cook, turning over halfway, for 10 minutes or until golden. Transfer to a plate. Cover to keep warm. Repeat with the remaining bread and silverbeet mixture to make 8 fingers.

4 Serve the fingers with tzatziki, lemon wedges, and scattered with mint, if desired.

COOK'S TIP

Mountain bread is very thin wrap bread. You'll find it with the other wraps at the supermarket.

NUTRITION (EACH)

CALS	FAT	SAT FAT	PROTEIN	CARBS
144	10g	5g	9g	5g

○ FREEZABLE ● KID FRIENDLY ○ MAKE AHEAD ○ SPEEDY ● VEGO

APRICOT CHICKEN DIPPERS

A fresh take on that old entertaining favourite takes sausage rolls to a new level of fun as the ultimate party food.

MAKES 12 **PREP** 25 mins **COOK** 45 mins

500g chicken mince
40g pkt French onion soup mix
20g (⅓ cup) panko breadcrumbs
⅓ cup chopped fresh coriander
90g (¼ cup) apricot jam
2 tbs Moroccan seasoning
2 green shallots, chopped
2 garlic cloves, crushed
3 sheets frozen puff pastry,
   just thawed
1 egg, lightly beaten

APRICOT DIPPING SAUCE
170g (½ cup) apricot jam
1 tbs apple cider vinegar
2 tsp sriracha
1 tsp grated fresh ginger

1 Place chicken, soup mix, breadcrumbs, coriander, jam, seasoning, shallot and garlic in a bowl. Season with pepper. Mix well to combine.

2 Preheat a sausage roll maker. Cut pastry sheets in half. Brush edges of 1 pastry half with egg. Leaving a 1cm edge, spoon ⅓ cup chicken mixture along 1 long side of the pastry. Roll up to enclose filling. Brush top with egg. Repeat with remaining pastry halves, egg and chicken mixture.

3 Place 4 pastry logs in sausage roll maker. Close lid. Cook for 12-14 minutes or until golden and cooked through. Transfer to a plate. Repeat with remaining pastry logs.

4 Meanwhile, to make the apricot dipping sauce, place all ingredients in a small saucepan over medium heat. Cook, stirring, until jam is melted. Bring to a simmer. Simmer for 3-5 minutes until thickened slightly. Remove from heat.

5 Serve the apricot chicken dippers warm with dipping sauce on the side.

COOK'S TIP

If you have any dippers left over, seal tightly in freezer bags with the air expelled and freeze for up to 2 months. To serve, thaw at room temperature and reheat in a moderate oven.

NUTRITION (EACH)

CALS	FAT	SAT FAT	PROTEIN	CARBS
265	11g	6g	12g	28g

● FREEZABLE ○ KID FRIENDLY ● MAKE AHEAD ○ SPEEDY ○ VEGO

MEATBALL PIZZA SUBS

A filling snack in under 25 minutes is ideal for hungry hordes. The kids will love this imaginative, delicious spin on meatballs.

MAKES 4 **PREP** 10 mins **COOK** 15 mins

4 x 20cm round wraps
12 (240g) small pork & beef meatballs
2 tbs pizza sauce, heated
55g (½ cup) grated mozzarella
Basil leaves, to serve (optional)

1 Place 3 meatballs close together in a row on each wrap, in the centre one-third of the way in from the front edge.

2 Working 1 at a time, fold the front edge of the wrap over the meatballs, then fold in the sides and roll up to enclose. Spray all over with oil. Place into 1 well of the sausage roll maker seam-side down (it might not fit neatly).

3 Close the lid, turn on the sausage roll maker and cook for 10 minutes. Open the lid and spoon sauce over the top of each sub. Sprinkle with cheese. Prop the lid open with the handle of a wooden spoon, to create a gap of about 2cm. Cook for a further 1-2 minutes until the cheese has melted. Season. Serve warm, scattered with basil leaves, if using.

COOK'S TIP

You can use any size raw meatballs for this recipe. Just use 60g (¼ cup) meatball mixture per sub – shaped to fit.

NUTRITION (EACH)

CALS	FAT	SAT FAT	PROTEIN	CARBS
302	16g	6g	15g	23g

○ FREEZABLE　● KID FRIENDLY　○ MAKE AHEAD　● SPEEDY　○ VEGO

10
minutes
prep

PORK & CABBAGE
DIM SIMS

Forget fiddly rice-paper wrappers. These sausage rolls are great Asian-style crowd-pleasers for your next do.

MAKES 16 **PREP** 20 mins **COOK** 1 hour

500g pork mInce
200g savoy cabbage, shredded
1 small carrot, grated
1 celery stick, finely chopped
2 green shallots, chopped
2 garlic cloves, crushed
2 tsp grated fresh ginger
1 tbs soy sauce
2 tsp sesame oil
4 sheets puff pastry, just thawed
1 egg, lightly beaten
Sweet and sour sauce, to serve

1 Place the pork, cabbage, carrot, celery, shallot, garlic, ginger, soy sauce and oil in a bowl. Season. Using your hands, mix well to combine.

2 Preheat a sausage roll maker. Cut pastry sheets in half. Brush edges with egg. Spoon ⅓ cup pork mixture along 1 long side of each pastry half about 1cm in from edge. Roll up to enclose filling. Brush tops with egg.

3 Place 4 pastry logs in sausage roll maker. Close the lid. Cook for 12-14 minutes or until golden and cooked through. Transfer to a plate and cover with a tea towel to keep warm. Repeat with remaining pastry logs to make 16.

4 Serve the dims sims immediately with sweet and sour sauce on the side.

COOK'S TIP

To make these a bit spicier, add a little finely chopped chilli to the pork mixture.

NUTRITION (EACH)

CALS	FAT	SAT FAT	PROTEIN	CARBS
220	12g	6g	9g	17g

● FREEZABLE ○ KID FRIENDLY ● MAKE AHEAD ○ SPEEDY ○ VEGO

FIVE-INGREDIENT LASAGNE ROLLS

Make the most of leftover spag bol by spinning it into tasty sausage rolls, ideal for a quick lunch or filling snack.

MAKES 8 **PREP** 10 mins **COOK** 30 mins

1 cup leftover cooked
dried spaghetti
1 cup leftover bolognese mixture
1 cup pre-grated pizza cheese
2 tbs chopped fresh continental
parsley, plus extra, to serve
(optional)
2 pieces mountain bread, quartered

1 Combine the pasta, bolognese mixture, cheese and parsley in a bowl.

2 Working quickly, arrange half of the pasta mixture along the bottom edge of 4 pieces of mountain bread. Tuck in the sides and roll to enclose. Place seam side down in the sausage roll maker. Spray with oil. Close the lid and turn on. Cook, turning over halfway, for 12-14 minutes Transfer to a plate and cover to keep warm. Repeat with the remaining bread and pasta mixture.

3 Serve the pasta rolls scattered with extra parsley, if desired.

COOK'S TIP

Add anything you fancy to these – chopped olives, mushrooms, or even a spoonful of pesto.

NUTRITION (EACH)

CALS	FAT	SAT FAT	PROTEIN	CARBS
129	6g	3g	9g	9g

★★★★★ *Clever! Great use of leftovers. My teenage son loves whipping a few of these up after sport on the weekend.* **RONSAUSGE**

○ FREEZABLE ● KID FRIENDLY ○ MAKE AHEAD ○ SPEEDY ○ VEGO

SPINACH & FETA GOZLEME

You can now make this popular market stall snack at home using your sausage roll maker. Our version uses much less oil too!

MAKES 8 **PREP** 15 mins **COOK** 25 mins

1 tbs extra virgin olive oil
2 green shallots, chopped
1 garlic clove, finely chopped
280g baby spinach
430g tub feta cubes
  in brine, drained
2 sheets frozen puff pastry,
  just thawed
Lemon cheeks and mint sprigs
  (optional), to serve

1 Heat the oil in a large frying pan over medium-high heat. Add the shallot and garlic. Cook, stirring, for 1 minute or until softened. Add the spinach. Cook, stirring occasionally, for 2 to 3 minutes or until just wilted.

2 Add feta. Season. Cook, stirring gently, for 30 seconds. Transfer to a sieve to drain. Set aside to cool for 5 minutes.

3 Preheat a sausage roll maker. Cut each sheet of pastry into quarters. Divide half the feta mixture between 4 pastry squares. Roll up to enclose filling. Place in the sausage roll maker. Cook for 8-10 minutes or until golden and puffed. Transfer to a plate. Repeat with the remaining pastry and feta mixture.

4 Serve the gözleme immediately with lemon cheeks and the mint, if using.

COOK'S TIP

Don't let the pastry thaw too much or it will be hard to work with. Keep chilled between batches if necessary.

NUTRITION (EACH)

CALS	FAT	SAT FAT	PROTEIN	CARBS
308	22g	13g	14g	14g

★★★★★ *Delicious. Made to instructions, plus added a little chicken stock powder for taste and halved the recipe for the two of us. Will be making again for sure!* **KAERU**

○ FREEZABLE   ● KID FRIENDLY   ○ MAKE AHEAD   ○ SPEEDY   ● VEGO

15
*minutes
prep*

CUSTARD & APPLE
PIES

Make single-serve apple pies with no mess and no fuss.
Save time by prepping the custard a day or two in advance.

MAKES 12 **PREP** 20 mins (+ 15 mins chilling) **COOK** 35 mins

2 tbs custard powder
250ml (1 cup) milk
2 tbs caster sugar
800g can apple slices pie fruit
3 sheets frozen puff pastry,
  just thawed
40g butter, melted
Cinnamon sugar, to dust

1 Place the custard powder in a small saucepan and add 2 tablespoons milk. Stir until smooth. Add the remaining milk and the sugar. Cook over medium-low heat, stirring, for 1 minute or until mixture boils and thickens. Transfer to a bowl and set aside for 5 minutes, stirring occasionally, until cooled. Place in the fridge for 15 minutes or until set.

2 Place pie apple slices in a strainer over a bowl to drain excess liquid.

3 Cut pastry sheets in half. Place 1 half over the base of a sausage roll maker and gently press into the 4 wells. Spoon 1 tablespoon of custard into each well and top each with a level ¼ cup of pie apple. Lay another pastry half over the top. Close the lid. Turn on the sausage roll maker and cook for 10 minutes or until golden.

4 Turn off sausage roll maker and transfer pies to a wire rack. Leave lid open to allow sausage roll maker to cool a little (just warm is fine, but not hot). Use kitchen scissors to separate pies and trim pastry edges. Brush with butter and sprinkle with cinnamon sugar. Repeat with remaining ingredients to cook 2 more batches. Cool slightly. Serve.

COOK'S TIP

For a twist, omit the custard, add some berries to the apple filling and serve with ice-cream.

NUTRITION (EACH)

CALS	FAT	SAT FAT	PROTEIN	CARBS
228	12g	7g	3g	28g

● FREEZABLE ● KID FRIENDLY ● MAKE AHEAD ○ SPEEDY ● VEGO

CHOCOLATE ECLAIRS

These cream-filled pastries are easy to whip up in a sausage roll maker. Everyone will be asking for your secret recipe!

MAKES 8 **PREP** 30 mins (+ cooling & 30 mins setting) **COOK** 40 mins

60g butter, chopped
75g (½ cup) plain flour
3 eggs, lightly beaten
100g dark chocolate, melted
300ml thickened cream
2 tbs icing sugar
1 tsp vanilla extract

1 Combine butter and 125ml (½ cup) water in a small saucepan and bring to the boil over medium heat. Add flour and stir until combined and smooth. Cook, stirring, for 2 minutes or until mixture forms a ball.

2 Transfer to an electric mixer fitted with the beater attachment. Beat for 2 minutes to cool slightly. Add egg in 3 batches, beating after each addition until well combined (the mixture should be smooth and glossy). Evenly divide half the mixture among the wells of the sausage roll maker. Close the lid and turn on the sausage roll maker. Cook for 18 minutes or until golden brown. Some mixture may ooze out, but don't worry.

3 Turn off the sausage roll maker. Leaving to lid open to allow the machine to cool a little, transfer eclairs to a wire rack. Use kitchen scissors to separate eclairs and trim the edges, then pierce a long hole through 1 end of each eclair to let steam escape. Repeat to make 4 more eclairs. Cool completely.

4 Dip tops of eclairs into melted chocolate and allow excess to drip off. Set aside for about 30 minutes until chocolate is set. Use electric beaters to whip cream, icing sugar and vanilla until firm peaks form. Transfer to a piping bag fitted with a 1cm plain nozzle. Pipe cream into the hole at the end of each eclair until full. Serve at room temperature or chilled.

NUTRITION (EACH)

CALS	FAT	SAT FAT	PROTEIN	CARBS
328	27g	17g	5g	16g

○ FREEZABLE ● KID FRIENDLY ○ MAKE AHEAD ○ SPEEDY ● VEGO

PANCAKE-WRAPPED MARS BARS

Deep-fried Mars bars are sooo yesterday. These bars are wrapped in fluffy pancakes and melted into a gooey, delicious dessert treat.

MAKES 4 **PREP** 10 mins **COOK** 5 mins

50g (⅓ cup) self-raising flour
1 tbs caster sugar
1 egg
60ml (¼ cup) milk
½ tsp vanilla extract (optional)
4 chilled Mars Bars
Icing sugar, to dust
Vanilla ice-cream or double cream, to serve (optional)

1 Preheat a sausage roll maker. Use a fork to combine the flour and sugar in a small bowl. Make a well in the centre and add the egg. Gently whisk the egg. Gradually whisk in the milk, incorporating the flour mixture, until the batter is smooth. Stir in the vanilla extract, if using.

2 Pour 2 teaspoons of the batter into each hole of the sausage roll maker. Place Mars bars on top. Pour over another 2 teaspoons of the batter to cover. Close the lid. Cook for 5 minutes or until golden. Transfer to a plate.

3 Dust the pancakes with icing sugar and serve warm with ice-cream or cream, if desired.

COOK'S TIP

It's important that the Mars Bars are chilled, so they melt to just the right degree during cooking.

NUTRITION (EACH)

CALS	FAT	SAT FAT	PROTEIN	CARBS
333	11g	5g	5g	53g

○ FREEZABLE ● KID FRIENDLY ○ MAKE AHEAD ● SPEEDY ● VEGO

10
minutes
prep

SWAP IT OUT
Looking for a tropical twist?
Substitute the Mars bars with Bounty bars
for a hit of coconut.

127

EASIEST-EVER CREAMY
VANILLA SLICE

Whip up a batch of these retro favourite pastries
for an elegant tea party, or just because you love them.

MAKES 8 **PREP** 15 mins (+ 20 mins chilling) **COOK** 25 mins

2 sheets frozen butter puff pastry,
    just thawed
300ml thickened cream
250ml (1 cup) milk
100g pkt vanilla instant pudding mix
Icing sugar, to dust
Strawberries, halved, to serve
    (optional)

1 Cut 1 sheet of pastry in half and stack the halves to make
a double layer. Place over base of a sausage roll maker
(leave flat) and close the lid. Turn on the sausage roll maker
and cook for 12 minutes or until golden. Lift out onto a wire
rack to cool, and repeat with remaining pastry sheet.

2 Meanwhile, place cream and milk in a large bowl and
sprinkle with the pudding mix. Using electric beaters,
beat for 2 minutes (it may look grainy). Cover and place in
the fridge for at least 20 minutes.

3 Use kitchen scissors to separate and trim pastry into
sections. Using a small sharp knife and starting at a
short end, carefully split pastry into top and bottom pieces.

4 Stir vanilla pudding mixture until smooth then transfer
to a piping bag fitted with a fluted nozzle. Pipe over half
the pastry pieces. Add pastry tops. Dust with icing sugar.
Serve with strawberries, if you like.

COOK'S TIP

These slices can
be assembled up
to 2 hours in
advance and
refrigerated until
serving time.

NUTRITION (EACH)

CALS	FAT	SAT FAT	PROTEIN	CARBS
343	23g	15g	4g	29g

○ FREEZABLE ● KID FRIENDLY ● MAKE AHEAD ○ SPEEDY ● VEGO

AIR FRYER

HATE DEEP-FRYING? HAVE WE GOT THE APPLIANCE
FOR YOU! THESE RECIPES ARE ALL ABOUT
THE NEW HEALTHIER WAY OF COOKING.

FRENCH-FRIED ZUCCHINI

You'll never have to miss out on fries again with this healthier zucchini version served with zesty tahini sauce.

SERVES 4 **PREP** 15 mins **COOK** 10 mins

45g (¼ cup) polenta
20g (¼ cup) finely grated parmesan
½ tsp finely grated lemon rind
1 egg
500g zucchini, cut into batons
1 tbs tahini
1½ tbs lemon juice
1 tbs extra virgin olive oil
2 tbs Greek-style yoghurt
1 garlic clove, crushed

1 Combine polenta, parmesan and lemon rind in a large bowl. Season. Lightly beat the egg in a bowl. Add the zucchini and toss to coat. Transfer zucchini mixture to polenta mixture and toss until zucchini is completed coated.

3 Place zucchini in an air fryer basket, discarding any excess polenta in base of bowl. Cook at 180°C, shaking basket halfway through, for 10 minutes or until zucchini is golden and just tender.

4 Meanwhile, use a fork to whisk the tahini and lemon juice in a bowl until smooth. Whisk in 1 tablespoon water. Whisk in oil, then yoghurt and garlic. Season.

5 Serve zucchini fries immediately with tahini dipping sauce on the side.

COOK'S TIP

Season the polenta mixture with a sprinkling of paprika as well as salt and pepper for a flavour kick.

NUTRITION (PER SERVE)

CALS	FAT	SAT FAT	PROTEIN	CARBS
1178	11g	2.6g	7g	11g

○ FREEZABLE ○ KID FRIENDLY ○ MAKE AHEAD ● SPEEDY ● VEGO

SWAP IT OUT

*If zucchini is out of season, try green beans or carrots.
Both work equally well.*

TOMATO & CHEESE TARTS

Make cheesy tarts in under half an hour using this easy recipe. They're a perfect dinner party starter.

SERVES 4 **PREP** 15 mins **COOK** 10 mins

1 sheet frozen puff pastry,
   just thawed
2 roma tomatoes, halved, sliced
2 tbs small basil leaves
120g bocconcini, torn or
   50g goat's cheese In oll
1 tbs extra virgin olive oil
Mixed salad leaves, to serve

1 Cut the pastry into 4 squares. Line four 8.5cm (base measurement) fluted tart tins with pastry squares. Cut off and discard excess pastry. Use a fork to prick base of tart.

2 Place 2 tins in an air fryer basket. Insert separating grill and add 2 remaining tins. Cook at 200°C for 6 minutes or until golden and puffed. Transfer tins to a board. Using a clean tea towel, carefully press down centre of tarts. Return tins to the air fryer. Cook for a further 2 minutes or until crisp.

3 Meanwhile, place tomato and basil in a bowl. Season and toss to combine.

4 Transfer tart shells to serving plates. Arrange tomato mixture in the shells. Top with cheese. Drizzle with olive oil and season. Serve with mixed leaves.

COOK'S TIP

Add a dash of balsamic vinegar to the tomato and basil mixture for extra zing.

NUTRITION (PER SERVE)

CALS	FAT	SAT FAT	PROTEIN	CARBS
354	25g	10g	11g	22g

○ FREEZABLE   ○ KID FRIENDLY   ○ MAKE AHEAD   ● SPEEDY   ● VEGO

15
minutes
prep

135

ZUCCHINI & HALOUMI FRITTERS

These family-friendly and easy fritters, packed with vegies and haloumi, will be your new weeknight winner.

SERVES 4 **PREP** 10 mins **COOK** 25 mins

- 2 zucchini, coarsely grated
- 225g block haloumi, coarsely grated
- 150g (1 cup) frozen corn kernels, thawed
- 2 eggs, lightly whisked
- 100g (⅔ cup) self-raising flour
- 3 tsp finely chopped fresh oregano leaves, plus extra sprigs, to serve
- Extra virgin olive oil, to drizzle (optional)
- Natural yoghurt, to serve

1 Use hands to squeeze out the excess liquid from the zucchini. Place in a bowl. Add the haloumi and corn and stir to combine. Make a well in the centre and add the egg, flour and oregano. Season and stir until well combined.

2 Drop tablespoonfuls of zucchini mixture onto the grill of an air fryer. Cook at 200°C for 8 minutes or until crisp and golden. Transfer to a plate and cover to keep warm. Repeat with the remaining mixture in 2 more batches.

3 Arrange fritters on a serving plate. Place the yoghurt in a small serving bowl. Season the yoghurt with black pepper and drizzle with olive oil, if using. Serve scattered with extra oregano.

COOK'S TIP

Serve the fritters with a tomato salsa instead of yoghurt for a tangy change.

NUTRITION (PER SERVE)

CALS	FAT	SAT FAT	PROTEIN	CARBS
330	14g	7.4g	21g	29g

★★★★★ *Delicious! Made these for lunch. Need to be cooked in the air fryer as they puff up. Tasty and whole family enjoyed. Yoghurt, as suggested, went well with them.* **LISACOOKS**

○ FREEZABLE ○ KID FRIENDLY ● **MAKE AHEAD** ○ SPEEDY ● **VEGO**

HEALTHIER SOUTHERN CHICKEN

Love crumbed chicken? This healthier version has all of the flavour with none of the extra oil.

SERVES 4 **PREP** 20 mins (+ 6 hours chilling) **COOK** 20 mins

2 chicken drumsticks, skin removed
2 chicken thigh cutlets, skin removed
250ml (1 cup) buttermilk
100g (⅔ cup) self-raising flour
1 tsp garlic powder
1 tsp onion flakes
1 tsp smoked paprika
200g red cabbage, thinly shredded
200g green cabbage, thinly shredded
1 carrot, coarsely grated
2 green shallots, finely chopped
⅓ cup coarsely chopped mint leaves
90g (⅓ cup) light Greek-style yoghurt
1 tbs Dijon mustard
1 garlic clove, crushed

1 Using a sharp knife, make 2 slits (to the bone) through the thickest part of the chicken drumsticks and cutlets. Place in a bowl and cover with buttermilk. Cover and chill for 6 hours or overnight.

2 Combine flour, garlic powder, onion flakes and paprika in a shallow bowl. Season.

3 Lightly spray an air fryer basket with oil. Working with 1 piece of chicken at a time, drain excess buttermilk then roll all over in flour mixture to coat. Place in the basket. Lightly spray chicken pieces with oil. Cook at 180°C for 20 minutes or until cooked through.

4 Meanwhile, combine cabbages, carrot, shallot and mint in a large bowl. Combine yoghurt, mustard and garlic in a jug. Season. Pour yoghurt mixture over vegetable mixture and toss to coat. Serve chicken with coleslaw.

COOK'S TIP

Air fry more chicken by using the separating grill and arranging the chicken in 2 layers in the basket.

NUTRITION (PER SERVE)

CALS	FAT	SAT FAT	PROTEIN	CARBS
636	20g	6g	80g	31g

○ FREEZABLE ○ KID FRIENDLY ○ MAKE AHEAD ○ SPEEDY ○ VEGO

FOUR-INGREDIENT
BROWNIE

It's time to try this decadent, big round brownie,
full of the flavours of hazelnut and chocolate.

SERVES 8 **PREP** 15 mins (+ cooling) **COOK** 40 mins

150g (1 cup) plain flour
225g (1 cup) white sugar
3 eggs, lightly whisked
300g (1 cup) Nutella
Cocoa powder, to dust (optional)

1 Lightly grease a 20cm round cake pan. Line the base with baking paper.

2 Sift the flour and sugar into a bowl. Make a well. Add the egg and Nutella to the well. Use a large metal spoon to stir until combined. Transfer to the prepared pan and smooth the top.

3 Place pan in an air fryer. Bake at 160°C for 40 minutes or until a skewer inserted into the centre comes out with a few crumbs sticking. Set aside to cool completely.

4 Dust with cocoa powder, if using, and cut into wedges to serve.

COOK'S TIP

Add a handful of finely chopped hazelnuts if you like extra crunch.

NUTRITION (PER SERVE)

CALS	FAT	SAT FAT	PROTEIN	CARBS
398	13g	4.1g	7g	64g

○ FREEZABLE   ○ KID FRIENDLY   ○ MAKE AHEAD   ○ SPEEDY   ○ VEGO

SECRET HACK

Cut through the richness of this brownie by serving it accompanied by a raspberry coulis and double cream.

VEGETARIAN PUMPKIN SCHNITZEL

No-one has to miss out on a classic pub favourite thanks to this delicious vegetarian schnitty recipe.

SERVES 4 **PREP** 30 mins **COOK** 15 mins

500g potatoes, peeled, cut into 3-4cm pieces

250g swede or turnip, peeled, cut into 3-4cm pieces

2½ tbs extra virgin olive oil

25g (½ cup) panko breadcrumbs (see tip)

25g (¼ cup) finely grated cheddar

2 tbs finely chopped hazelnuts

1 tbs finely chopped continental parsley leaves, plus extra leaves, to serve

1 egg

500g butternut pumpkin, peeled, cut into 1cm-thick slices

Lemon wedges, to serve

1 Place potato and turnip in a medium saucepan and cover with water. Season with salt. Bring to the boil over high heat. Simmer, covered, for 15 minutes or until tender. Drain well and return to pan. Add 2 tablespoons oil, season and mash until smooth.

2 Meanwhile, combine breadcrumbs, cheddar, hazelnut, parsley and remaining oil in a shallow dish. Season. Lightly beat the egg on a shallow plate.

3 One at a time, dip pumpkin slices into egg to coat. Place in the breadcrumb mixture and press all over to coat. Place in an air fryer basket, using the grill separator to arrange a second layer of coated pumpkin when needed. Cook at 180°C for 12 minutes or until golden and tender.

4 Arrange pumpkin schnitzels and mash on serving plates. Sprinkle with extra parsley. Serve with lemon wedges.

COOK'S TIP

Look for panko breadcrumbs in the Asian food section of the supermarket. They will add great texture.

NUTRITION (PER SERVE)

CALS	FAT	SAT FAT	PROTEIN	CARBS
644	26g	4.8g	19g	90g

○ FREEZABLE ○ KID FRIENDLY ○ MAKE AHEAD ○ SPEEDY ● VEGO

30
minutes
prep

MAPLE MUSTARD PORK BELLY

Impress your guests with sweet and tangy pork belly, topped with a rind cooked to crispy air fryer perfection.

SERVES 6 **PREP** 10 mins (+ resting) **COOK** 1 hour 10 mins

1kg pork belly, scored, patted dry
2 tbs maple syrup
2 tsp wholegrain mustard, plus
    extra, to serve
2 tsp apple cider vinegar
2 tsp finely chopped fresh rosemary,
    plus extra sprigs, to serve

1 Season pork rind well with salt, rubbing into the scores. Arrange on the grill of an air fryer. Cook at 200°C for 20 minutes or until the rind starts to crackle.

2 Meanwhile, combine the maple syrup, mustard, vinegar and rosemary in a bowl.

3 Reduce air fryer to 180°C. Roast the pork for a further 30 minutes or until the rind is well crackled and the flesh is tender. Brush with the maple syrup mixture. Cook for 10 minutes or until the rind is dark golden. Transfer to a plate and set aside for 10 minutes to rest.

4 Cut into pieces. Scatter with rosemary sprigs and serve with extra mustard.

COOK'S TIP

To ensure crisp crackling, unwrap the pork belly and leave uncovered in the fridge overnight for the skin to dry out.

NUTRITION (PER SERVE)

CALS	FAT	SAT FAT	PROTEIN	CARBS
417	28g	10g	34g	7g

★★★★★

*I've lost count of how many times I've made this.
So delicious and a winner with the family!*

RACHEALNEILSON

○ FREEZABLE ○ KID FRIENDLY ○ MAKE AHEAD ○ SPEEDY ○ VEGO

QUICK CHICKEN FRIED RICE

For a healthier take on this family fave, try our air fryer fried rice. It will hit the hunger spot in no time.

SERVES 4 **PREP** 10 mins **COOK** 20 mins

300g chicken tenderloins
4 rashers rindless bacon
450g pkt microwave
    long-grain rice
2 tbs oyster sauce
2 tbs light soy sauce
1 tsp sesame oil
3 tsp finely grated fresh ginger
2 eggs, lightly whisked
120g (¾ cup) frozen peas
2 green shallots, sliced
1 long fresh red chilli, thinly sliced
Oyster sauce, to drizzle

1 Place the chicken and bacon on the grill of an air fryer. Cook at 180°C for 8 minutes or until cooked through. Transfer to a plate and set aside to cool slightly. Slice the chicken and chop the bacon.

2 Meanwhile, use your fingers to separate the rice grains in the packet. Microwave rice for 1 minute. Transfer to a 20cm round, high-sided ovenproof dish or cake pan. Add the oyster sauce, soy sauce, sesame oil, ginger and 2 tablespoons water. Stir to combine.

3 Place dish or pan in the air fryer. Cook for 5 minutes or until rice is tender. Stir in the egg, peas, chicken and half the bacon. Cook for 3 minutes or until egg is cooked through. Stir in half the shallot. Season with salt and white pepper.

4 Serve sprinkled with chilli, remaining shallot, remaining bacon and extra oyster sauce to drizzle.

COOK'S TIP

This is a great dish to use up leftover cooked chicken and vegetables. Just toss chopped vegies in with the egg.

NUTRITION (PER SERVE)

CALS	FAT	SAT FAT	PROTEIN	CARBS
186	11g	6.8g	9g	11g

○ FREEZABLE ○ KID FRIENDLY ○ MAKE AHEAD ● SPEEDY ○ VEGO

CRUMBED CHICKEN TENDERS

How do you make these easy crumbed tenderloins the crispest ever?
Simply coat them in cheesy corn chips, that's how!

SERVES 4 **PREP** 15 mins (+ 4 hours marinating) **COOK** 20 mins

500g chicken tenderloins,
  halved crossways
250ml (1 cup) buttermilk
170g packet cheese corn chips
1 egg
50g (⅓ cup) plain flour
Mild salsa, to serve

1 Place chicken in a glass or ceramic bowl. Cover with the buttermilk. Cover and place in the fridge for 4 hours or overnight to marinate.

2 Pulse the corn chips in a food processor until coarsely chopped. Transfer to a shallow bowl. Whisk the egg in another shallow bowl. Place the flour on a plate.

3 Drain the chicken and discard the buttermilk. Working with a few pieces at a time, coat the chicken in the flour, shaking to remove excess. Dip in the egg and then place in the corn chips, pressing well to coat. Spray with oil.

4 Place half the chicken in an air fryer. Bake at 180°C for 8-10 minutes or until golden and cooked through. Repeat with remaining chicken. Serve immediately with salsa.

COOK'S TIP

Use any flavour of corn chips you like. Even plain corn chips will taste great!

NUTRITION (PER SERVE)

CALS	FAT	SAT FAT	PROTEIN	CARBS
459	17g	7g	37g	37g

○ FREEZABLE ● KID FRIENDLY ○ MAKE AHEAD ○ SPEEDY ○ VEGO

EASY BANANA MUFFINS

These easy-peasy banana muffins are super fluffy and moist, and make great on-the-go treats.

MAKES 18 **PREP** 10 mins **COOK** 20 mins

2 ripe bananas
150g (1 cup) self-raising flour
60g (⅓ cup lightly packed) brown sugar
1 egg
60ml (¼ cup) olive oil
60ml (¼ cup) buttermilk
Maple syrup, to brush, plus extra (optional), to serve

1 Use a fork to mash the bananas in a small bowl. Set aside until required.

2 Whisk the flour and sugar in a medium bowl. Make a well. Add the egg, oil and buttermilk to the well. Stir until combined. Stir through the banana.

3 Divide half of the mixture among 9 patty cases. Place on the grill of an air fryer. Cook at 180°C for 8-10 minutes or until muffins are cooked through. Transfer to a wire rack. Repeat with the remaining mixture to make 18 muffins.

4 Brush tops of the muffins with maple syrup while still warm. Serve with extra maple syrup, if you like.

COOK'S TIPS

You'll need 18 paper patty cases for this recipe. Store the muffins in an airtight container for up to 3 days.

NUTRITION (EACH)

CALS	FAT	SAT FAT	PROTEIN	CARBS
92	3.5g	0.6g	1.5g	13g

★★★★★

First time making muffins in an air fryer. These turned out great! My kids loved them! **MILLATRIX**

● FREEZABLE ● KID FRIENDLY ● MAKE AHEAD ● SPEEDY ● VEGO

SMOKY CHIPOTLE CHICKEN EMPANADAS

You won't be able to resist these South American-style pastries, packed with spiced chicken, olives and fragrant coriander.

MAKES 16 **PREP** 20 mins (+ cooling) **COOK** 45 mins

2 tbs olive oil

400g chicken thigh fillets, fat trimmed

1 brown onion, finely chopped

2 garlic cloves, crushed

1 tsp plain flour

1 tsp ground cumin

½ tsp ground coriander

½ tsp sweet paprika

125ml (½ cup) chicken stock or water

1 hard-boiled egg, coarsely chopped

¼ cup finely chopped fresh coriander

225g (¾ cup) smoky chipotle mayonnaise

4 sheets frozen ready-rolled shortcrust pastry, just thawed

16 small pitted Sicilian olives

1 egg, lightly beaten

1. Heat 1 tablespoon oil in a large frying pan over medium heat. Add the chicken and cook, turning, for 8 minutes or until browned. Transfer to a plate and set aside until cool enough to handle. Finely shred the chicken.

2. Heat the remaining oil in the pan over medium heat. Add the onion and garlic and cook, stirring often, for 4 minutes or until softened. Add the flour, cumin, coriander and paprika. Cook, stirring, for 1 minute. Return chicken to the pan, add the stock or water and bring to the boil. Simmer for 2 minutes or until thickened slightly. Set aside to cool completely.

3. Stir the egg, coriander and ¼ cup of the mayonnaise into the chicken mixture. Season.

4. Using a round 10.5cm cutter, cut 16 rounds from the pastry. Place 1 tablespoon of chicken mixture and 1 olive in the centre of each round. Fold the pastry over to enclose the filling, forming half-moon shapes. Press the edges with a fork to seal. Brush with egg and season with salt.

5. Place half the empanadas on the grill of an air fryer. Cook at 180°C for 15 minutes. Transfer to a plate and cover with a tea towel to keep warm. Repeat with remaining empanadas. Serve warm with the remaining mayonnaise for dipping.

NUTRITION (EACH)

CALS	FAT	SAT FAT	PROTEIN	CARBS
318	24g	6g	4g	7g

○ FREEZABLE ○ KID FRIENDLY ● MAKE AHEAD ○ SPEEDY ○ VEGO

PORK & VEGETABLE SPRING ROLLS

Crispy spring rolls are so delicious. And when you can make them yourself for the hungry hordes at home, who needs take out?

MAKES 18 **PREP** 30 mins (+ cooling) **COOK** 20 mins

65g dried vermicelli noodles
1 tbs vegetable oil
250g pork mince
2 garlic cloves, crushed
3 tsp finely grated fresh ginger
1 carrot, peeled, coarsely grated
100g shiitake mushrooms, stalk removed, finely chopped
2 tsp cornflour
1 tbs cold water
2 tbs oyster sauce
1 tbs soy sauce
18 frozen spring roll wrappers, thawed
Sweet and sour sauce, and thinly sliced green shallots, to serve

1 Soak the noodles in boiling water for 3 minutes or until softened. Drain and refresh under cold water, squeezing out any excess moisture. Cut into 5cm lengths. Set aside.

2 Heat oil in a wok over medium-high heat. Add pork. Cook, stirring, for 2-3 minutes, until browned. Add garlic and ginger. Cook, stirring, for 1 minute. Stir in carrot, mushroom and noodles. Whisk cornflour and water in a jug until smooth. Add oyster sauce, soy sauce and half the cornflour mixture to the wok. Cook, stirring, for 1-2 minutes, until combined and liquid is absorbed. Set aside to cool.

3 Place 1 spring roll wrapper, with a corner closest to you, on a clean work surface. Place 2 heaped tablespoons pork mixture in the centre. Fold in the sides, then fold over the bottom corner. Spread a little remaining cornflour mixture over top corner, then roll up from the bottom to enclose the filling and form a log. Repeat to make 18 spring rolls.

4 Spray spring rolls with oil. Place one-third on the grill of an air fryer. Cook at 200°C for 3-4 minutes, until crisp. Transfer to a plate lined with paper towel and cover with a tea towel to keep warm. Repeat for remaining 2 batches.

5 Sprinkle spring rolls with shallot and serve warm with sweet and sour sauce.

COOK'S TIP

Covering cooked spring rolls with a tea towel allows them to stay warm while also remaining crispy.

NUTRITION (EACH)

CALS	FAT	SAT FAT	PROTEIN	CARBS
100	4g	0.8g	4g	12g

○ FREEZABLE ● KID FRIENDLY ○ MAKE AHEAD ○ SPEEDY ○ VEGO

SHREDDED CHICKEN TAQUITOS

Filled with barbecue chicken, our crispy, crunchy taquitos are great for a quick and easy Mexican dinner.

SERVES 8 **PREP** 20 mins **COOK** 15 mins

1 barbecued chicken
2 green shallots, finely chopped
¼ cup chopped fresh coriander
1 tsp ground cumin
1 tsp dried oregano
8 large wholemeal tortillas
4 cups shredded iceberg lettuce
2 tomatoes, finely chopped
½ small red onion, finely chopped
Finely grated parmesan, to serve
Chipotle chilli sauce, to serve
Light sour cream, to serve
Guacamole dip, to serve
Fresh coriander leaves, to serve

1 Remove skin and meat from the chicken. Discard bones. Use 2 forks to shred the meat and finely slice the skin. Transfer the meat and skin to a large bowl. Add the shallot, coriander, cumin and oregano. Season. Stir well to combine.

2 Place 1 tortilla on a clean work surface. Top with ¾ cup chicken mixture. Brush edge with water. Roll up firmly to enclose filling, pressing the edge to seal. Transfer to a tray, seam side down. Repeat with remaining chicken mixture and tortillas to make 7 more.

3 Place 4 of taquitos, seam-side down, in the basket of an air fryer. Cook at 180°C for 6 minutes or until crisp and golden. Transfer to a plate and cover with foil to keep warm. Repeat with the remaining 4 taquitos.

4 Spread lettuce over a serving platter. Top with the taquitos. Scatter with tomato and onion and sprinkle with parmesan. Drizzle with chipotle, sour cream and guacamole. Serve immediately.

COOK'S TIP

For extra crispy taquitos, spray with a little oil before cooking.

NUTRITION (PER SERVE)

CALS	FAT	SAT FAT	PROTEIN	CARBS
557	28g	8g	35g	38g

○ FREEZABLE ○ KID FRIENDLY ○ MAKE AHEAD ○ SPEEDY ○ VEGO

CORN CHIP CRUMBED
HALOUMI

Serve these delicious chips as finger food at a party or as a side dish for a casual dinner.

MAKES 28 **PREP** 30 mins (+ 15 mins chilling) **COOK** 10 mins

170g packet cheese corn chips
40g (¼ cup) plain flour
2 eggs
2 x 180g packets haloumi, rinsed
Chopped continental parsley leaves,
 to serve (optional)
ROASTED CAPSICUM DIP
330g jar roasted whole peppers,
 rinsed, drained
2 tbs sour cream

1 Place the corn chips in a food processor and process until fine crumbs form. Transfer to a shallow dish. Place flour in a shallow bowl and whisk the eggs in another shallow bowl.

2 Line a baking tray with baking paper. Cut each block of haloumi into 14 chips. Coat in the flour, shaking off excess. Dip in egg then in the crumbs, pressing firmly to coat. Transfer to prepared tray and place in the fridge for 15 minutes to chill.

3 Meanwhile, to make the roasted capsicum dip, place the peppers and sour cream in a clean food processor and process until smooth. Season. Transfer mixture to a small serving dish or bowl.

4 Place half the haloumi chips in an air fryer basket. Cook at 180°C for 5-6 minutes, until crisp. Season. Set aside and cover with a tea towel to keep warm. Repeat with remaining chips.

5 Serve haloumi chips immediately with the capsicum dip, and sprinkled with parsley, if using.

COOK'S TIP

If you want a quicker dipping sauce, serve with a jar of Mexican tomato salsa.

NUTRITION (EACH)

CALS	FAT	SAT FAT	PROTEIN	CARBS
85	5g	2.6g	4g	7g

○ FREEZABLE ○ KID FRIENDLY ○ MAKE AHEAD ○ SPEEDY ● VEGO

SWAP IT OUT
*Switch cheese corn chips with gluten-free plain corn chips
and flour with gluten-free flour to make it suitable
for the gluten intolerant.*

INDIAN-SPICED CAULIFLOWER

Roasted cauliflower takes on a spicy flavour in this recipe, which can be served as a delicious side or vegetarian main.

SERVES 4 **PREP** 10 mins **COOK** 20 mins

1 tsp cumin seeds
1 tsp coriander seeds
¾ tsp sea salt flakes
Pinch of turmeric
1 (about 600g) cauliflower, trimmed, cut into florets
Raita (see tip) or coconut yoghurt, to serve
Extra virgin olive oil, to drizzle
Fresh mint leaves, to serve

1 Combine the cumin, coriander, salt and turmeric in a mortar. Crush with a pestle to a coarse mixture. Transfer to a bowl. Add the cauliflower and toss to coat.

2 Place half the coated cauliflower in single layer on the grill of an the air fryer. Cook at 180°C for 8 minutes or until tender. Transfer to a serving bowl and cover to keep warm. Repeat with the remaining coated cauliflower.

3 Place the raita or yoghurt in a small bowl and drizzle with olive oil. Serve cauliflower with the raita or yoghurt and scattered with mint leaves.

COOK'S TIP

Make a super-quick raita by adding a little chopped fresh mint and coriander plus a sprinkling of garam masala to your favourite coconut yoghurt.

NUTRITION (PER SERVE)

CALS	FAT	SAT FAT	PROTEIN	CARBS
89	6g	3g	3g	5g

★★★★★

Simple and delicious. Will definitely be making this again in the future. **ARINANASYITAH**

○ FREEZABLE   ○ KID FRIENDLY   ○ MAKE AHEAD   ● SPEEDY   ● VEGO

BROCCOLI & BACON CROQUETTES

Golden crunchy broccoli croquettes pair perfectly
with tangy blue cheese dipping sauce.

SERVES 10 (as a starter) **PREP** 30 mins (+ 15 mins chilling) **COOK** 40 mins

600g potatoes, peeled, chopped
350g broccoli, chopped
  into small florets
4 rindless bacon rashers,
  finely chopped
4 green shallots, thinly sliced
60g vintage cheddar,
  coarsely grated
1 egg yolk
255g (1½ cups) plain flour
2 eggs
155g (2½ cups) fresh breadcrumbs

BLUE CHEESE DIPPING SAUCE
125g (½ cup) sour cream
60g firm blue cheese, crumbled
1 tbs buttermilk

1 Cook the potato in a saucepan of boiling water for 12-15 minutes, until tender. Drain well. Use a potato masher to mash until smooth. Transfer to a large bowl.

2 Meanwhile, cook broccoli in a saucepan of boiling water for 5 minutes or until tender. Drain. Set aside. When cool enough to handle, finely chop.

3 Heat a non-stick frying pan over medium heat. Cook the bacon, stirring, for 3 minutes. Add the shallot and cook for 3 minutes or until the bacon is crispy and shallot is softened. Drain on paper towel.

4 Add broccoli, bacon mixture, cheddar, egg yolk and 40g (¼ cup) flour to the potato. Season and stir to combine. Roll heaped tablespoonfuls of mixture into croquette shapes and place on a tray lined with baking paper.

5 Whisk the eggs in a shallow bowl. Place the breadcrumbs and remaining flour on separate plates. Coat each croquette in flour, then dip in egg and roll in the breadcrumbs. Place on prepared tray. Cover and place in the fridge for 15 minutes.

6 Meanwhile, for the dipping sauce, use a stick blender to pulse the sour cream and cheese in a small bowl until combined. Add the buttermilk. Process until just combined. Season.

7 Place one-third of the croquettes in an air fryer. Spray with oil. Cook at 180°C, turning halfway, for 8 minutes or until golden. Transfer to a plate and cover to keep warm. Repeat with the remaining croquettes in 2 more batches. Serve warm with the dipping sauce.

NUTRITION (PER SERVE)

CALS	FAT	SAT FAT	PROTEIN	CARBS
294	11g	6g	14g	32g

● FREEZABLE ○ KID FRIENDLY ● MAKE AHEAD ○ SPEEDY ○ VEGO

★★★★★
Great for a party.
These little gems were gone in no time.
So easy to make. **CATHIE R**

MEXICAN-STYLE
SAUSAGE ROLLS

Packed with hidden vegies and sprinkled with cheese,
these quick and easy sausage rolls will be a new family fave.

MAKES 20 **PREP** 20 mins **COOK** 25 mins

1 tbs olive oil
1 small brown onion, finely chopped
1 carrot, peeled, coarsely grated
1 zucchini, trimmed, coarsely grated
500g pork and beef mince
30g (⅓ cup) dried breadcrumbs
30g packet taco spice mix
2 sheets frozen puff pastry,
   just thawed
1 egg, lightly whisked
30g (¼ cup) finely grated cheddar
Mashed avocado, to serve
Lime, halved, juiced, plus extra lime
   halves, to serve (optional)
Coriander sprigs, to serve (optional)
Mild salsa, to serve

1 Heat the oil in a frying pan over medium heat. Add the onion and cook, stirring often, for 2 minutes or until slightly softened. Add the carrot and zucchini. Cook, stirring often, for 3 minutes or until softened. Set aside to cool slightly before transferring to a food processor. Process until smooth.

2 Place the mince in a large bowl. Add pureed vegetables, breadcrumbs and spice mix. Use your hands to mix until well combined. Divide the mixture into 4 equal portions.

3 Line a tray with baking paper. Lay 1 sheet of pastry on a work surface and cut in half. Arrange 1 portion of meat mixture along 1 long edge of the pastry. Brush the other long edge with egg. Roll to enclose meat mixture, making sure pastry overlaps by about 1cm. Cut into 5 even pieces. Place, seam side down, on prepared tray. Repeat with remaining pastry and filling. Brush tops of the rolls with remaining egg.

4 Place half the sausage rolls on the grill of an air fryer. Cook at 180°C for 6 minutes. Sprinkle with cheese and cook for a further 2 minutes. Transfer to a plate and cover with a tea towel to keep warm. Repeat with the remaining sausage rolls.

5 Combine the avocado with lime juice and top with coriander, if you like. Serve sausage rolls with the salsa and avocado dip.

COOK'S TIP

If you are not concerned with hiding the vegetables, omit the processing and combine the cooked vegies with the other ingredients in step 2.

NUTRITION (EACH)

CALS	FAT	SAT FAT	PROTEIN	CARBS
146	8g	3.7g	8g	9g

○ FREEZABLE ○ KID FRIENDLY ● MAKE AHEAD ○ SPEEDY ○ VEGO

LEMON RICOTTA DESSERT CAKE

Made from fresh ricotta, this baked cake has a similar texture to cheesecake and is delicious served with lemon curd and vanilla ice-cream.

SERVES 8 **PREP** 20 mins **COOK** 40 mins

125g butter, at room
   temperature, chopped
155g (¾ cup) caster sugar
1 lemon, rind finely grated
250g fresh ricotta
3 eggs
150g (1 cup) self-raising flour
60ml (¼ cup) fresh lemon juice
100g (¼ cup) lemon curd,
   plus extra, to serve
Pure icing sugar, to dust
Vanilla ice cream, to serve

1 Grease a 20cm springform cake pan and line the base with baking paper.

2 Using electric beaters, beat the butter, sugar and lemon rind until pale and creamy. Add the ricotta and beat until just combined. Add the eggs, 1 at a time, beating well after each addition.

3 Use a large metal spoon to fold the flour into the mixture. Stir in the lemon juice. Transfer mixture to the prepared pan and dollop with lemon curd. Use a flat bladed knife to swirl the lemon curd into the batter. Gently tap the pan on the bench to settle the batter.

4 Place the cake pan in an air fryer. Cook at 150°C for 35-40 minutes or until a skewer inserted into the cake comes out clean (see tip).

5 Cool cake in the pan for 10 minutes, then release and transfer to a serving plate. Dust with icing sugar and serve warm, topped with extra curd and ice-cream.

COOK'S TIP

When you test the cake, try to avoid the lemon swirls on top. Placing the skewer in these parts can give a 'wetter' outcome and you run the risk of overcooking.

NUTRITION (PER SERVE)

CALS	FAT	SAT FAT	PROTEIN	CARBS
486	24g	15g	9g	61g

○ FREEZABLE ○ KID FRIENDLY ○ MAKE AHEAD ○ SPEEDY ○ VEGO

★ ★ ★ ★ ★

Made my own curd using
a taste.com.au recipe. The cake is super easy
to make but seems more sophisticated.

LUSHSTICK

JAFFLES & TOASTIES

NOT JUST FOR KIDS, THIS SANDWICH-WITH-BENEFITS
HAS BEEN REINVENTED FOR A NEW GENERATION.

BACON-WRAPPED BREKKIE SANDWICH

Heat up the jaffle press for this modern twist on an old standby. Combine baked beans with avocado and bacon for a super tasty snack.

SERVES 2 **PREP** 10 mins **COOK** 5 mins

20g butter, softened
4 slices white bread
4 slices streaky bacon
½ avocado, thinly sliced
⅓ cup baked beans
Sriracha chilli sauce, to drizzle

1 Preheat the jaffle maker. Spread butter over 1 side of each slice of bread. Lay 1 slice of bacon on an angle in each hole of jaffle maker. Top each with 1 slice of bread, buttered-side down. Divide the avocado between the 2 jaffles, then the beans. Drizzle with sriracha. Sandwich with remaining bread slices, buttered-side up.

2 Top jaffle with remaining bacon. Close lid. Cook for 4 minutes or until golden. Serve.

COOK'S TIP

If you don't have sriracha, try a dash of Worcestershire sauce or a sprinkle of paprika instead.

NUTRITION (PER SERVE)

CALS	FAT	SAT FAT	PROTEIN	CARBS
516	33g	14g	16g	36g

HEALTHY HACK

Switch white bread to wholegrain, streaky bacon to lean ham and butter to olive oil spray for a healthier version.

○ FREEZABLE ○ KID FRIENDLY ○ MAKE AHEAD ● SPEEDY ○ VEGO

TUNA & SWEET CORN MELTS

These family favourites get a handy twist in a jaffle maker.
With just 10 minutes prep time, you can fill hungry tummies in a snap.

SERVES 2 **PREP** 10 mins **COOK** 5 mins

95g can tuna in olive oil,
   drained, flaked
35g (⅓ cup) grated cheddar
125g can corn kernels, drained
6 slices bread-and-butter pickles,
   finely chopped
¼ red onion, finely chopped
1 tbs Japanese-style mayonnaise
1 tbs chopped fresh continental
   parsley leaves, plus extra sprigs,
   to serve
20g butter, softened
4 slices white bread

1 Preheat the jaffle maker. Combine tuna, cheese, corn,
pickles, onion, mayonnaise and parsley in a bowl. Season.

2 Spread butter over 1 side of each slice of bread. Place
1 slice of bread, buttered-side down, in each hole of the
jaffle maker. Top evenly with tuna mixture. Sandwich with
remaining bread slices, buttered-side up. Close the lid.
Cook for 4 minutes or until golden and cheese is melted.
Serve with extra parsley.

COOK'S TIP

Add a little
chopped fresh
chilli for extra zing,
if you like.

NUTRITION (PER SERVE)

CALS	FAT	SAT FAT	PROTEIN	CARBS
474	26g	12g	21g	38g

HEALTHY HACK

*Switch white bread to wholegrain and butter
to olive oil spray to make this a little healthier.*

○ FREEZABLE ● **KID FRIENDLY** ○ MAKE AHEAD ● **SPEEDY** ○ VEGO

SUPER-EASY, CHEESY PIZZAS

Toss in all your favourite pizza toppings for a quick and easy handheld meal. Everyone will love these.

SERVES 2 **PREP** 10 mins **COOK** 5 mins

4 slices white bread
20g butter, softened
2 tbs tomato paste
4 slices salami, torn
¼ cup roasted capsicum strips
8 small pitted kalamata olives
40g (⅓ cup) grated mozzarella
Dried oregano, to sprinkle

1 Preheat the jaffle maker. Spread 1 side of each slice of bread with butter. Turn bread over. Spread the other side of the bread with tomato paste.

2 Place 1 slice of bread, buttered-side down, in each hole of the jaffle maker. Top with salami, capsicum, olives and mozzarella. Sandwich with remaining bread slices, buttered-side up. Sprinkle with oregano. Close lid. Cook for 4 minutes or until golden and cheese is melted. Season. Serve.

COOK'S TIP

Other favourite pizza topping combos work just as well, such as ham and pineapple, four cheeses, or tomato, basil and goat's cheese.

NUTRITION (PER SERVE)

CALS	FAT	SAT FAT	PROTEIN	CARBS
362	19g	10g	15g	32g

SWAP IT OUT

To make this suitable for the gluten-intolerant, swap bread with gluten-free varieties and ensure you use gluten-free salami.

○ FREEZABLE ○ KID FRIENDLY ○ MAKE AHEAD ● SPEEDY ○ VEGO

10
minutes
prep

FIVE-A-DAY VEGIE
QUESADILLAS

Cooked in a sandwich press, these quick and easy quesadillas are loaded with black beans, cheese and vegies.

SERVES 4 **PREP** 20 mins **COOK** 20 mins

400g can black beans, rinsed, drained

420g can corn kernels, drained

1 red capsicum, deseeded, finely chopped

140g (1 cup) grated butternut pumpkin

60g baby spinach, shredded

4 green shallots, thinly sliced

8 flour tortillas

160g (2 cups) grated cheddar, plus extra, to sprinkle

Bought tomato salsa, to serve

Sour cream, to serve

Fresh coriander sprigs, to serve

Lemon wedges, to serve

1 Combine the beans, corn, capsicum, pumpkin, spinach and shallot in a large mixing bowl. Season well.

2 Preheat a sandwich press. Spray 1 side of a tortilla with oil and place oil-side down on a chopping board. Sprinkle with ¼ cup cheddar, then top with ½ cup of the vegetable mixture. Fold over. Sprinkle the top with a little extra cheddar.

3 Place the quesadilla in the sandwich press. Close the lid and cook for 2 minutes or until golden. Transfer to a chopping board and cut into wedges. Repeat with remaining tortillas, cheese and vegetable mixture to make 7 more quesadillas. Dollop with salsa and sour cream. Sprinkle with coriander sprigs and serve with lemon wedges.

NUTRITION (PER SERVE)

CALS	FAT	SAT FAT	PROTEIN	CARBS
714	33g	18g	29g	72g

COOK'S TIP

You can also cook quesadillas in a large non-stick frying pan over medium-high heat. Cook, pressing down firmly with a spatula, for 1-2 minutes each side or until golden and crisp.

○ FREEZABLE ○ KID FRIENDLY ○ MAKE AHEAD ○ SPEEDY ● VEGO

★★★★★

Both my husband and son liked these! Healthy, easy and delicious. Thank you. **TCART**

HAM, CHEESE & GARLIC BREAD STACKS

Need some comfort food? Make these luxurious toasties in a sandwich press in just a few minutes.

MAKES 4 **PREP** 5 mins **COOK** 5 mins

½ baguette, ends trimmed, cut into 8 slices
60g garlic butter, at room temperature (see tip)
60g thinly sliced smoked leg ham
80g gruyere, coarsely grated
Finely chopped fresh continental parsley, to serve

1 Preheat a sandwich press. Spread 4 slices of bread with half the garlic butter. Turn over and top with the ham and cheese. Spread garlic butter over remaining bread slices and place on top of the stack, butter-side up.

2 Place sandwiches in press. Cook for 5 minutes or until golden and the cheese is melted.

3 Cut the ham and cheese sandwiches in half. Sprinkle with parsley to serve.

COOK'S TIP

You can find garlic butter in the chilled section of the supermarket.

NUTRITION (PER SERVE)

CALS	FAT	SAT FAT	PROTEIN	CARBS
383	10g	11g	16g	33g

○ FREEZABLE ○ KID FRIENDLY ○ MAKE AHEAD ● SPEEDY ○ VEGO

★★★★★

IMOGENR

5
minutes
prep

179

CHEESY MAPLE BACON JAFFLE

The perfect snack-for-one, this jaffle is loaded with maple syrup and bacon and ready in just 15 minutes.

SERVES 1 **PREP** 5 mins **COOK** 10 mins

2 thick slices white bread
30g butter, at room temperature
2 tsp wholegrain mustard
60g cheddar, thinly sliced
2 thin bacon rashers (see tip)
Maple syrup, to drizzle

1 Spread 1 side of each slice of bread with butter. Turn bread over, spread 1 slice with mustard and arrange cheese slices on top.

2 Preheat a jaffle maker. Lightly spray 1 bacon rasher with oil. Place oiled-side down into a hole of the jaffle maker (across the cutting edge in the centre). Place the mustard and cheese-topped bread, buttered-side up, on top of the bacon. Top with remaining bread slice, buttered-side up, then lay the remaining bacon rasher on top. Lightly spray the bacon with oil.

3 Cook, checking occasionally, for 5-6 minutes until golden. Drizzle with maple syrup to serve.

COOK'S TIP

Thicker slices of bacon may need a slightly longer cooking time.

NUTRITION (PER SERVE)

CALS	FAT	SAT FAT	PROTEIN	CARBS
755	50g	31g	36g	39g

○ FREEZABLE   ○ KID FRIENDLY   ○ MAKE AHEAD   ● SPEEDY   ○ VEGO

5 minutes prep

SWAP IT OUT
Try mozzarella to make the cheesy filling extra oozy and creamy.

EASY JAFFLE-MAKER
APPLE PIE

With only five ingredients, including puff pastry and cooked apple filling, you can make this classic dessert in just 25 minutes.

MAKES 2 **PREP** 5 mins **COOK** 20 mins

1 sheet frozen puff pastry,
  just thawed
225g (1 cup) cooked apple (see tip)
20g butter, melted
Cinnamon sugar, to sprinkle
Thick vanilla custard, to serve

1 Preheat the jaffle maker. Cut the pastry sheet into quarters. Spread the apple onto 2 of the quarters, leaving a 1.5cm border. Top with the remaining pastry quarters.

2 Place in the jaffle maker and close the lid. Cook for 15 minutes or until the pastry is golden.

3 Carefully transfer the jaffles to a wire rack to cool slightly. Brush with melted butter, sprinkle with cinnamon sugar and serve immediately with custard.

COOK'S TIP

You can use canned pie fruit apple slices to make this dessert quick and easy. Any leftover apple can be frozen for future use.

NUTRITION (PER SERVE)

CALS	FAT	SAT FAT	PROTEIN	CARBS
470	26g	16g	6.7g	50g

○ FREEZABLE ○ KID FRIENDLY ○ MAKE AHEAD ● SPEEDY ● VEGO

SWAP IT OUT

This is a great basic recipe for any fruit pie
cooked in a jaffle maker. Try pear or rhubarb to change it up a little.

THE ULTIMATE ROAST PORK JAFFLE

Why wait for lefover roast pork just to make a jaffle? These delicious sandwiches, served with slaw, are a whole meal.

SERVES 4 **PREP** 25 mins **COOK** 5 hours 15 mins

2kg pork shoulder
2 tsp salt
250ml (1 cup) hot water
8 slices white bread
Butter, to spread
Smoked barbecue sauce, to spread
Fresh continental parsley
   leaves, to serve
COLESLAW
300g savoy cabbage,
   finely shredded
2 carrots, finely shredded
3 green shallots, trimmed, sliced
125g (½ cup) chipotle mayonnaise

1 Preheat the oven to 250°C/230°C fan forced. Use a very sharp knife to cut deep scores into the pork rind, slicing nearly to the flesh. Rub with salt, ensuring salt gets into scores. Place pork in a roasting dish. Roast for 30 minutes or until rind starts to crackle. Reduce heat to 170°C/150°C fan forced. Baste pork with pan juices. Pour hot water around pork. Cover with baking paper and foil. Bake for 4½ hours or until tender. Increase heat to 250°C/230°C fan forced. Cook for 10 minutes or until crackling is crisp. Remove crackling from pork. Break into pieces. Use tongs and a fork to shred meat.

2 For the coleslaw, combine the cabbage, carrot and shallot in a bowl. Add mayonnaise and toss to combine.

3 Preheat a jaffle maker. Butter 2 slices of bread. Spread 1 buttered slice with barbecue sauce. Top with pork and remaining bread slice. Cook in jaffle maker until golden. Repeat with remaining bread, butter, sauce and pork. Scatter with parsley and serve with coleslaw and crackling.

COOK'S TIP

Smoked barbecue sauce is an easy ingredient for adding smoky, sweet and salty flavour.

NUTRITION (PER SERVE)

CALS	FAT	SAT FAT	PROTEIN	CARBS
1133	74g	22g	82g	34g

○ FREEZABLE ○ KID FRIENDLY ○ MAKE AHEAD ○ SPEEDY ○ VEGO

25 minutes prep

SWAP IT OUT
Use hoisin sauce instead of barbecue to give this dish an Asian twist.

TOASTED SALMON BURRITOS

Flavour salmon fillets with Mexican spices and wrap up a delicious meal in around half an hour.

SERVES 6 **PREP** 10 mins **COOK** 20 mins

800g skinless salmon fillets
30g pkt Mexican spice mix
1 tbs sesame seeds
6 wholegrain wraps
½ iceberg lettuce, shredded
1 large carrot, peeled,
    coarsely grated
140g grated cheddar
2 avocados, thinly sliced
1 cup fresh coriander sprigs
½ cup garlic aioli

1 Cut salmon into 1cm-thick slices. Place Mexican spice mix and sesame seeds in a large sealable plastic bag. Add salmon. Seal. Toss to coat.

2 Heat a non-stick frying pan over medium-high heat. Spray with oil. Cook salmon, in batches, for 1-2 minutes each side, until cooked.

3 Preheat a sandwich press. Lay out the wraps and place salmon mixture in the centre of each. Evenly divide the lettuce, carrot, cheddar, avocado, coriander and aioli among the wraps. Fold in the sides and roll to enclose.

4 Cook the burritos, 1 at a time, in the sandwich press for 1-2 minutes, until crisp and light golden. Cut in half. Serve.

COOK'S TIP

You can swap the salmon for firm white fish fillets, chicken tenderloins or strips of tofu, if you like.

NUTRITION (PER SERVE)

CALS	FAT	SAT FAT	PROTEIN	CARBS
828	56g	14g	44g	33g

○ FREEZABLE   ○ KID FRIENDLY   ○ MAKE AHEAD   ● SPEEDY   ○ VEGO

★★★★★

A winner.

SKHILLIER1

MINI MEXICAN TOASTED BITES

These snack-size cheese sandwiches are not too spicy, so they're a fast and easy after-school tummy filler.

SERVES 4 **PREP** 10 mins **COOK** 5 mins

1 avocado, peeled, chopped
2 tsp lemon juice
8 mini flour tortillas
2 x 125g cans kidney beans, rinsed and drained
⅓ cup mild chunky salsa
35g (⅓ cup) grated reduced-fat cheddar

1 Preheat a sandwich press. Mash the avocado and lemon juice together in a bowl until almost smooth. Season. Spread 4 tortillas with avocado mixture. Top with beans, salsa, cheese and remaining tortillas.

2 Place 2 tortilla stacks in the sandwich press. Cook for 1-2 minutes until golden and heated through. Set aside on a plate and cover with foil to keep warm. Repeat with remaining 2 tortilla stacks. Cut into quarters. Serve.

NUTRITION (PER SERVE)

CALS	FAT	SAT FAT	PROTEIN	CARBS
369	21g	6g	10g	33g

COOK'S TIP

To make this a meal, serve with a salad of baby cos lettuce, grape tomatoes and sliced cucumber. You could replace one can of beans with ⅔ cup of shredded cooked chicken.

★★★★★ *Very fast and easy. Served with sour cream, extra guacamole and salsa on top. Yummy!* **COOKIESMAMA**

○ FREEZABLE ○ KID FRIENDLY ○ MAKE AHEAD ● SPEEDY ● VEGO

10
minutes
prep

GREEK-STYLE CHICKEN YIROS

A flat yiros sandwich is also known as a skepasti. This version is so speedy to assemble and cook, it's the ultimate fast food.

SERVES 2 **PREP** 10 mins **COOK** 5 mins

150g chicken breast, cooked and chopped
1 capsicum, chargrilled, skin removed, thinly sliced
2 tbs sundried tomatoes, thinly sliced
50g Greek feta, crumbled
40g (½ cup) grated cheddar
1 tbs fresh oregano leaves, coarsely chopped
4 yiros bread rounds

1 Put the chicken, capsicum, tomato, feta, cheddar and oregano in a bowl and toss to combine.

2 Preheat a sandwich press. Lay 2 bread rounds on a flat surface. Divide chicken mixture between rounds. Top with remaining bread rounds.

3 Place in the sandwich press. Toast for 2-3 minutes until cheese has melted and filling is heated through. Cut into quarters. Serve.

NUTRITION (PER SERVE)

CALS	FAT	SAT FAT	PROTEIN	CARBS
1019	40g	13g	59g	101g

COOK'S TIP

If you have a sandwich press at work, you can assemble these and wrap in foil to take with you. Keep refrigerated then cook at lunchtime.

SECRET HACK

Try other flatbreads such as tortillas, if yiros are not available.

○ FREEZABLE ○ KID FRIENDLY ● MAKE AHEAD ● SPEEDY ○ VEGO

SPEEDY TOASTED BEEF
TACOS

This recipe puts a twist on your favourite taco flavours and serves up a flat-out dinner winner.

SERVES 4 **PREP** 5 mins **COOK** 15 mins

1 red onion, thinly sliced into rounds
60ml (¼ cup) white wine vinegar
1 tsp caster sugar
1 tbs extra virgin olive oil
500g lean beef mince
1 red capsicum, finely chopped
1 carrot, coarsely grated
30g sachet salt-reduced taco
   spice mix
250ml (1 cup) tomato puree
8 flour tortillas
140g (1⅓ cups) grated pizza cheese
2 green shallots, thinly sliced
½ cup fresh coriander leaves
90g (⅓ cup) sour cream

1 Combine the onion, vinegar and sugar with a large pinch of salt and 60ml (¼ cup) water in a small bowl. Set aside.

2 Heat the oil in a large frying pan over high heat. Cook beef and capsicum, breaking up beef with a wooden spoon, for 5 minutes or until browned. Add capsicum, carrot and spice mix. Cook, stirring, for 1 minute. Add tomato puree. Cook, stirring, for 1 minute or until heated through. Set aside.

3 Preheat a sandwich press. Lay 4 tortillas on a clean work surface. Divide beef mixture among tortillas. Top with cheese, then remaining tortillas. Place 2 tortillas in the sandwich press. Cook for 2 minutes or until golden and crisp. Set aside and cook remaining 2 tortillas.

4 Meanwhile, drain the onion mixutre. Sprinkle tacos with pickled onion, shallot and coriander. Serve with sour cream on the side.

COOK'S TIP

If you don't have a large sandwich press, you can make these smaller by covering half the tortilla with filling, then folding over to enclose.

NUTRITION (PER SERVE)

CALS	FAT	SAT FAT	PROTEIN	CARBS
807	40g	9g	50g	58g

○ FREEZABLE ○ KID FRIENDLY ○ MAKE AHEAD ● SPEEDY ○ VEGO

EASY BREKKIE
TOASTIE

This simple toastie is full of vegies (with a hit of protein) to get a busy day off to a good start in next to no time.

SERVES 4 **PREP** 15 mins **COOK** 10 mins

4 pieces wholemeal Lebanese bread
250g fresh low-fat ricotta
40g rocket leaves
Olive oil spray
4 eggs
1 x 250g punnet cherry tomatoes, quartered
½ red onion, finely chopped
1 fresh long red chilli, halved, deseeded, thinly sliced
2 tbs chopped fresh coriander leaves
1 tbs fresh lime juice
Fresh coriander leaves, to serve

1 Preheat a sandwich press. Place the bread on a clean work surface. Spread ricotta over half of each piece of bread. Top with rocket. Fold in half to enclose filling. Spray with olive oil spray. Put 1 sandwich into the sandwich press and cook for 2 minutes or until toasted. Transfer to a plate and cover with foil to keep warm. Repeat with the remaining sandwiches.

2 Spray a non-stick frying pan with olive oil spray. Heat over medium heat. Crack in the eggs and cook for 3 minutes or until cooked to your liking.

3 Meanwhile, combine the tomato, onion, chilli, chopped coriander and lime juice in a bowl. Cut the quesadillas into wedges. Divide among serving plates. Top with eggs, salsa and coriander leaves. Season and serve.

COOK'S TIP

If you don't have a sandwich press, you can cook the quesadillas in a non-stick frying pan for 1-2 minutes each side.

NUTRITION (PER SERVE)

CALS	FAT	SAT FAT	PROTEIN	CARBS
355	10g	3.5g	21g	45g

○ FREEZABLE   ○ KID FRIENDLY   ○ MAKE AHEAD   ● SPEEDY   ● VEGO

★★★★★

Variation: I put the salsa in the flat bread and served with poached egg and a dollop of sour cream. Yummo.

JULIEIMMONEN

15 minutes prep

MEXICAN-STYLE VEGIE TORTILLAS

Pickled chillies add a kick to the salsa, and complement the sweet pumpkin, in this budget-busting weeknight dinner.

SERVES 4 **PREP** 20 mins **COOK** 35 mins

850g Kent pumpkin, peeled, cut into 1.5cm pieces
2 tbs extra virgin olive oil
1 small red onion, finely chopped
2 garlic cloves, crushed
2 tsp ground cumin
400g can chickpeas, rinsed, drained
⅔ cup fresh coriander leaves, coarsely chopped
100g low-fat feta, crumbled
55g (1 cup) reduced-fat cheddar, finely grated
8 wholegrain tortillas
250g baby tomato medley, chopped
30g drained pickled jalapeño chillies
Reduced fat sour cream, to serve

1 Preheat the oven to 200°C/180°C fan forced. Line a baking tray with baking paper. Place pumpkin on tray. Spray with olive oil. Season. Roast, stirring halfway, for 15-20 minutes until golden and tender.

2 Heat 1 tablespoon of oil in a large non-stick frying pan over medium-low heat. Add onion and cook, stirring, for 3 minutes or until soft. Stir in garlic and cumin for 1 minute or until aromatic. Stir in chickpeas for 2 minutes or until warmed through. Coarsely crush with a potato masher. Add pumpkin to pan and stir until combined. Remove from heat and stir in half the coriander. Season.

3 Preheat a large sandwich press. Combine feta and cheddar in a bowl. Brush tortillas with remaining oil, turn 4 over and sprinkle with half the cheese mixture. Top with pumpkin mixture. Sprinkle with remaining cheese mixture and top with remaining tortillas oil-side up. Place a filled tortilla in the sandwich press. Close the lid. Cook for 1-2 minutes until golden. Transfer to a plate and cover with foil to keep warm. Cook remaining filled tortillas.

4 Meanwhile combine tomato, chilli and remaining coriander in a bowl. Season. Cut quesadillas into quarters. Top with tomato salsa and a dollop of sour cream. Drizzle with any remaining olive oil to serve.

NUTRITION (PER SERVE)

CALS	FAT	SAT FAT	PROTEIN	CARBS
635	29g	12g	26g	61g

○ FREEZABLE ○ KID FRIENDLY ○ MAKE AHEAD ○ SPEEDY ● VEGO

20 minutes prep

★★★★★

This was delicious. Very easy to make and could easily be modified for a bit of variety. **LSPOONER**

CHEESY PESTO & VEG
FLATBREADS

Put a delicious and veg-packed spin on toasties with these easy, cheesy flatbreads.

SERVES 4 **PREP** 15 mins **COOK** 40 mins

- 500g sweet potato, peeled, cut into 3cm pieces
- 1 large red onion, cut into wedges
- 1 tbs olive oil
- 150g broccoli, cut into small florets
- 8 flour tortillas
- 240g (3 cups) coarsely grated cheddar or mozzarella
- 85g (⅓ cup) sour cream
- 1-2 tbs pesto
- Baby rocket leaves, to serve

1 Preheat the oven to 200°C/180°C fan forced. Place the sweet potato and onion in a large roasting pan. Drizzle with oil and season. Roast for 20 minutes. Add broccoli to the pan. Toss. Roast for 10 minutes or until vegies are tender.

2 Preheat a large sandwich press. Spray tortillas with oil. Turn 4 over and sprinkle with half the cheese. Top with vegie mixture. Use a fork to gently mash. Sprinkle with remaining cheese. Top with remaining tortillas oil-side up. Place 1 filled tortilla on the sandwich press. Close the lid and cook for 1-2 minutes until golden. Transfer to a plate and cover with foil to keep warm. Cook remaining filled tortillas.

3 Swirl the sour cream through the pesto in a bowl (do not fully combine). Cut the flatbreads into quarters. Scatter with rocket and serve with a dollop of pesto cream.

COOK'S TIP

Use any leftover roasted vegies in these tortilla toasties.

NUTRITION (PER SERVE)

CALS	FAT	SAT FAT	PROTEIN	CARBS
767	44g	21g	27g	62g

○ FREEZABLE ○ KID FRIENDLY ○ MAKE AHEAD ○ SPEEDY ● VEGO

CHICKEN & SESAME
SATAY

Use pantry basics and a jaffle maker to turn leftover chicken into a sophisticated toasted sandwich with an Asian flavour.

SERVES 2   **PREP** 10 mins   **COOK** 5 mins

20g butter, softened
4 slices white bread
2 tbs crunchy peanut butter
1 tbs hoisin sauce, plus extra, to serve
1 cup leftover cooked shredded chicken
2 green shallots, thinly sliced
2 tbs grated cheddar
Sesame seeds, to sprinkle

1 Preheat a jaffle maker. Spread bread slices with butter on 1 side. Turn over. Spread with peanut butter, then hoisin sauce.

2 Place 1 slice of bread, buttered-side down, in each hole of the jaffle maker. Top with chicken, shallot and cheese. Sandwich with remaining bread slices, buttered-side up. Sprinkle with sesame seeds. Close lid. Cook for 4 minutes or until golden and cheese is melted. Serve with extra sauce.

COOK'S TIP

Swap the chicken for thinly sliced tofu or bean sprouts to make it vegetarian.

NUTRITION (PER SERVE)

CALS	FAT	SAT FAT	PROTEIN	CARBS
560	30g	11g	37g	33g

○ FREEZABLE   ● KID FRIENDLY   ○ MAKE AHEAD   ● SPEEDY   ○ VEGO

HEALTHY HACK
Swap white bread with wholegrain and lightly spray with olive oil instead of butter for a healthier version.

KALE, FETA & FRIED EGG QUESADILLA

Put a spicy spin on Mexican night with these delish quesadillas, packed with kale and cheesy goodness!

SERVES 4 **PREP** 20 mins **COOK** 25 mins

60ml (¼ cup) extra virgin olive oil
1 large brown onion, finely chopped
1 garlic clove, crushed
2½ tsp ground cumin
200g baby kale, plus extra
   to serve (optional)
1 lemon, rind finely grated, juiced
130g (1¼ cups) coarsely grated
   fresh mozzarella
150g smooth feta, crumbled
100g grape tomatoes, sliced
1 fresh long red chilli, thinly sliced
8 multigrain tortillas
4 eggs
Micro herbs, to serve (optional)

1 Preheat the oven to 120°C/100°C fan forced. Line 2 baking trays with baking paper.

2 Heat 1 tablespoon of oil in a non-stick frying pan over medium-low heat. Cook onion, stirring, for 4 minutes or until golden. Add garlic and 2¼ teaspoons of cumin. Cook, stirring, for 1 minute or until aromatic. Add kale and cook, stirring, for 4 minutes or until wilted. Stir in lemon rind and 1 tablespoon of juice. Season. Transfer to a bowl. Set aside for 5 minutes to cool. Stir in cheeses.

3 Meanwhile, combine the tomato, chilli, 1 tablespoon lemon juice and 2 teaspoons of oil in a bowl. Season. Set aside until ready to serve.

4 Preheat a large sandwich press. Brush tortillas with olive oil. Turn 4 over and spread with kale mixture. Top with remaining tortillas oil-side up. Place 1 quesadilla in the sandwich press. Close the lid. Cook for 1-2 minutes until golden. Transfer to prepared tray and keep warm in oven. Cook remaining quesadillas.

5 Heat remaining oil in a non-stick pan over medium heat. Sprinkle remaining cumin into the pan. Crack eggs into pan. Cook, basting with oil once, for 3-4 minutes for soft yolks or until cooked to your liking.

6 Divide quesadillas among serving plates. Top with eggs, tomato mixture and extra kale and herbs, if using.

NUTRITION (PER SERVE)

CALS	FAT	SAT FAT	PROTEIN	CARBS
657	38g	15g	34g	41g

○ FREEZABLE ○ KID FRIENDLY ○ MAKE AHEAD ○ SPEEDY ● VEGO

LOW-CAL SPICY VEGO
TRIANGLES

These easy meat-free Mexican-style sandwiches are filled with spicy beans and salsa for a tastebud sensation.

SERVES 4 **PREP** 20 mins **COOK** 10 mins

1 small avocado, finely chopped
1 green shallot, finely chopped
1 tbs fresh lime juice
½ tsp sriracha chilli sauce
2 tbs chopped fresh coriander leaves
400g can no-added-salt red kidney
    beans, rinsed, drained
125g chargrilled capsicum,
    finely chopped
125g cherry tomatoes,
    finely chopped
40g (½ cup) coarsely grated cheddar
1 tsp salt-reduced taco seasoning
4 light flour tortillas
Lime wedges, to serve

JALAPEÑO & RADISH SALSA
4 large radishes, trimmed,
    finely chopped
1 fresh jalapeño chilli, deseeded,
    finely chopped
⅓ cup chopped fresh
    coriander leaves
1 lime, juiced

1 To make the jalapeño and radish salsa, combine all the ingredients in a bowl. Season.

2 Combine the avocado, shallot, lime juice, sriracha and 1 tablespoon coriander in a bowl. Season. Combine the kidney beans, capsicum, tomato, cheddar, taco seasoning and remaining coriander in a separate bowl. Season.

3 Preheat a sandwich press. Spray 1 side of each tortilla with oil. Turn over. Place a quarter of the bean mixture on half of each tortilla. Fold over remaining half to enclose.

4 Place 1 filled tortilla in the sandwich press. Close the lid. Cook for 1-2 minutes until golden. Set aside on a plate covered with foil to keep warm. Cook remaining filled tortillas.

5 Cut each filled tortilla in half. Serve with the jalapeño and radish salsa, avocado mixture and lime wedges.

COOK'S TIP

Use vegan cheese to make this dish vegan.

NUTRITION (PER SERVE)

CALS	FAT	SAT FAT	PROTEIN	CARBS
333	15g	4.5g	12g	31g

○ FREEZABLE ○ KID FRIENDLY ○ MAKE AHEAD ● **SPEEDY** ● **VEGO**

QUICK CHIPOTLE CHICKEN

WRAPS

These spicy chicken wraps are ready in around 30 minutes.
Serve them for dinner or as a weekend lunchtime treat.

SERVES 4 **PREP** 15 mins **COOK** 15 mins

400g can red kidney beans,
   rinsed, drained
300g chopped cooked chicken
1 small red capsicum, deseeded,
   finely chopped
2 green shallots, chopped
1-2 tsp smoky chipotle seasoning,
   to taste
150g pre-grated three cheese blend
6 large wholemeal wraps
50g baby spinach, plus extra,
   to serve
1 tomato, deseeded, finely chopped
¼ cup fresh coriander sprigs
1 lime, juiced
1 avocado, thinly sliced
Thick Greek-style yoghurt, to serve

1 Place the beans in a large bowl. Use a fork to lightly mash. Add chicken, capsicum, shallot and chipotle seasoning. Season and stir to combine.

2 Preheat a grill press. Spray 1 side of each wrap with oil. Turn over. Scatter half of the cheese over half of each wrap. Top with the bean mixture and spinach. Scatter with remaining cheese. Fold over remaining halves to enclose.

3 Place 1 filled wrap in the grill press. Close the lid and cook for 1-2 minutes until crisp, golden and the cheese has melted. Transfer to a plate and cover with foil to keep warm. Cook remaining filled wraps.

4 Meanwhile, combine tomato, coriander and lime juice in a bowl. Season. Cut wraps in half. Top with avocado, tomato salsa and extra spinach. Serve with yoghurt.

COOK'S TIP

These can also
be cooked in
a regular flat
sandwich press,
if that is what
you have.

NUTRITION (PER SERVE)

CALS	FAT	SAT FAT	PROTEIN	CARBS
777	32g	11g	47g	67g

○ FREEZABLE   ○ KID FRIENDLY   ○ MAKE AHEAD   ● **SPEEDY**   ○ VEGO

★ ★ ★ ★ ★

Such a nice recipe. I mixed chipotle sauce and Greek yoghurt. It was really lovely. **JASMINE PEMBERTON**

10-MINUTE BEAN TORTILLAS

So simple and packed with vegies, this healthy meal can be whipped up super fast. Perfect for a lunch-for-one.

SERVES 1 **PREP** 5 mins **COOK** 5 mins

100g rinsed, drained canned black beans or kidney beans (see tip)
30g chopped roasted red capsicum (not in oil)
1 tbs fresh ricotta
Hot chilli sauce, to taste (optional)
1 wholegrain tortilla
20g baby spinach leaves, plus extra, to serve

1 Place beans in a bowl. Use a fork to coarsely mash. Add the capsicum, ricotta and chilli sauce, if using. Stir to combine.

2 Preheat a sandwich press. Spray tortilla lightly with oil. Turn over and spread the bean mixture over half. Top with spinach leaves. Fold remaining half over to enclose. Place in the sandwich press and toast until golden. Serve with extra spinach leaves.

NUTRITION (PER SERVE)

CALS	FAT	SAT FAT	PROTEIN	CARBS
289	6g	3g	15g	37g

COOK'S TIP

This recipe can be adapted for meat-lovers by adding barbecued chicken.

SWAP IT OUT

Swap the tortilla with a gluten-free corn tortilla or wrap to make this recipe gluten free.

○ FREEZABLE ○ KID FRIENDLY ○ MAKE AHEAD ● SPEEDY ● VEGO

TOASTED CORNED BEEF REUBEN

Your favourite American deli-style sandwich is toasted to golden perfection in a sandwich press.

SERVES 4 **PREP** 15 mins **COOK** 20 mins

65g (¼ cup) reduced-fat plain Greek-style yoghurt
2 tsp tomato sauce
1½ tsp Worcestershire sauce
½ fresh long red chilli, finely chopped
250g green cabbage, finely shredded
8 thick slices rye bread
2 tbs olive oil
2 dill pickles, sliced
280g shaved silverside (corned beef)
6 slices Swiss cheese
Mixed salad leaves, to serve

1 Combine yoghurt, tomato sauce, Worcestershire and chilli in a large bowl. Add cabbage. Season. Toss to coat.

2 Brush 1 side of bread slices with oil. Top 4 slices bread, oil-side down, with pickles, silverside, cabbage mixture and cheese. Top with remaining bread slices, oil-side up.

3 Preheat a sandwich press. Place 1 sandwich in press. Cook for 4 minutes or until cheese starts to melt. Transfer to a plate and cover with foil to keep warm. Cook remaining sandwiches. Serve with salad leaves.

COOK'S TIP

Rye bread is traditional for a reuben sandwich, but use can use any bread you prefer.

NUTRITION (PER SERVE)

CALS	FAT	SAT FAT	PROTEIN	CARBS
700	29g	12g	41g	64g

★★★★★ *Yum yum yum – I could have this a couple times a week!* **CAITLINRENAE**

○ FREEZABLE   ○ KID FRIENDLY   ○ MAKE AHEAD   ○ SPEEDY   ○ VEGO

ROASTED VEGETABLES ON TURKISH

Give roasted vegetables a new lease on life with this easy vegetarian cheese toastie, perfect for lunch or a lazy dinner.

SERVES 4 **PREP** 10 mins **COOK** 25 mins

4 cups mixed vegetables (such as zucchini, capsicum, red onion, sweet potato, pumpkin, cauliflower), chopped
2 tbs extra virgin olive oil
150g tomato medley mix
240g (1 cup) quark, goat's cheese or fresh ricotta
2 tbs chopped fresh herbs (such as dill, parsley or basil), plus extra, to serve
½ Turkish loaf, halved horizontally
Balsamic glaze, to serve

1 Preheat oven to 180°C/160°C fan forced. Place the mixed vegies in a roasting pan. Drizzle with oil. Season. Roast for 10 minutes. Add tomatoes and roast for 10 minutes or until the vegetables are tender.

2 Meanwhile, combine the quark and herbs in a small bowl. Season.

3 Cut the Turkish loaf into 8 even pieces and lightly spray with oil. Preheat a grill press. Grill the bread, in 2 batches for 1-2 minutes until lightly charred.

4 Spread 4 bread pieces with the quark mixture. Top with roasted vegetables and extra herbs. Drizzle with balsamic. Top with remaining bread pieces and serve.

COOK'S TIP

To use up leftover roasted vegies in these panini, just reheat them in a moderate oven first.

NUTRITION (PER SERVE)

CALS	FAT	SAT FAT	PROTEIN	CARBS
331	12g	2.1g	15g	38g

○ FREEZABLE ○ KID FRIENDLY ○ MAKE AHEAD ○ SPEEDY ● VEGO

10
minutes
prep

★★★★★
Easy to make and delicious.
Even my fussy 6-year-old enjoyed it!. MANDY084

NUTELLA & CUSTARD PARCELS

The easiest dessert pastries ever, these sweet fruity toasties can also be served with cream or ice-cream.

SERVES 2 **PREP** 5 mins **COOK** 5 mins

4 slices raisin bread
20g butter, softened
2 tbs Nutella spread
2 tbs custard
1 tsp icing sugar
Chopped hazelnuts,
   to serve

1 Preheat a jaffle maker. Spread 1 side of each slice of bread with butter. Put 2 slices of bread, buttered-side down, in the jaffle maker. Spread a tablespoon of Nutella over each slice, then 1 tablespoon of custard. Top with remaining slices of bread, buttered-side up. Close the lid. Cook for 2 minutes or until golden.

2 Dust the toasties with icing sugar and scatter with hazelnuts to serve.

COOK'S TIP

If you don't have raisin bread, sprinkle a few sultanas or dried cranberries into the filling.

NUTRITION (PER SERVE)

CALS	FAT	SAT FAT	PROTEIN	CARBS
404	19g	8.3g	8.2g	50g

SWAP IT OUT

Give this recipe a European twist by using panettone, an Italian-style Christmas bread instead of raisin bread.

○ FREEZABLE ● KID FRIENDLY ○ MAKE AHEAD ● SPEEDY ● VEGO

CHEESE & HAM WAFFLE STACK

Crispy and buttery store-bought waffles make for great toasties!
Pack them with smoked ham and mozzarella for a savoury snack.

MAKES 6 **PREP** 10 mins **COOK** 25 mins

12 frozen waffles, thawed
155g (1½ cups) coarsely grated
 mozzarella
3-4 tomatoes, sliced
12 slices smoked ham

1 Preheat a sandwich press. Sprinkle 6 waffles with half the mozzarella. Top with tomato and ham. Sprinkle with remaining mozzarella. Top with the remaining waffles.
2 Place 2 waffle sandwiches in the sandwich press. Close the lid. Cook for 6-7 minutes until golden brown and the cheese is melted. Repeat in 2 more batches to make 6 sandwiches.

NUTRITION (EACH)

CALS	FAT	SAT FAT	PROTEIN	CARBS
216	10g	5g	17g	15g

COOK'S TIP

If you don't have
a sandwich press
or jaffle maker,
bake these on
a baking tray in
the oven at
200°C/180°C
fan forced instead.

★★★★★

*Genius! Adding the waffles takes an
ordinary ham and cheese toastie to next level!*

RONSAUSGE

○ FREEZABLE   ● **KID FRIENDLY**   ○ MAKE AHEAD   ○ SPEEDY   ○ VEGO

WAFFLE
MAKER

AIRY, FLUFFY AND JUST A LITTLE BIT DECADENT,
WAFFLES CAN TURN ANY MEAL OR DESSERT
INTO A SHOW-STOPPER.

CHOC-DRIZZLED CHURROS

These delicious Spanish street-food snacks are a hot favourite around the world, and now you can make them in your own kitchen.

SERVES 4 **PREP** 20 mins **COOK** 15 mins

2 eggs, separated
60ml (¼ cup) milk
100g butter, melted
1 tsp vanilla extract
200g (1⅓ cups) self-raising flour
2 tbs caster sugar
155g (¾ cup) sugar
1 tsp ground cinnamon

FUDGY CHOCOLATE SAUCE
200g milk chocolate, chopped
2 tbs brown sugar
80ml (⅓ cup) thickened cream

1 Preheat the oven to 150°C/130°C fan forced. Place a wire rack over a large baking tray and place in oven.

2 For the fudgy chocolate sauce, place the chocolate, sugar and cream in a saucepan over medium heat. Cook, stirring, for 5 minutes or until melted and smooth. Set aside for 5 minutes to cool.

3 Meanwhile, preheat a waffle maker. Whisk the egg yolks, milk, butter and vanilla in a bowl. Sift in the flour. Add the caster sugar and whisk until almost smooth. Using an electric mixer, beat the egg whites in a bowl until stiff peaks form. Add a quarter of the egg white to the batter, folding to combine. Add remaining egg white. Fold to combine.

4 Half-fill the waffle maker with batter. Close the lid. Cook for 1 minute 30 seconds or until golden and cooked through. Transfer to the wire rack in the oven to keep warm (see tip). Repeat with remaining batter in 3 more batches.

5 Remove waffles from oven. Combine the sugar and cinnamon in a dish. Toss each waffle in cinnamon mixture to lightly coat. Serve with chocolate sauce.

COOK'S TIP

Placing the waffles on a rack rather than straight on the tray while in the oven helps to keeps them crisp.

NUTRITION (PER SERVE)

CALS	FAT	SAT FAT	PROTEIN	CARBS
943	47g	29g	13g	120g

○ FREEZABLE ● KID FRIENDLY ○ MAKE AHEAD ○ SPEEDY ● VEGO

PEANUT BUTTER BERRY WAFFLES

We've given waffles a nutty upgrade with peanut butter chips. Your kids will love this take on a delicious ice-cream sundae.

SERVES 6 **PREP** 15 mins (+ cooling) **COOK** 30 mins

200g (1⅓ cups) self-raising flour
1 tbs caster sugar
2 eggs
330ml (1⅓ cups) milk
80g butter, melted
1 tsp vanilla extract
145g (1 cup) peanut butter chips
Icing sugar, for dusting
Vanilla ice-cream, to serve
2 tbs chopped peanuts, to serve

BERRY SAUCE
500g frozen raspberries
50g (¼ cup) caster sugar
250g strawberries, hulled, halved

1 Preheat the oven to 150°C/130°C fan forced. Place a wire rack over a baking tray and place in the oven.

2 For the berry sauce, place the raspberries and sugar in a large saucepan over medium-high heat. Cook, crushing raspberries with a wooden spoon, for 5 minutes or until sugar has dissolved. Bring to the boil. Reduce heat to medium-low. Simmer for 5 minutes or until mixture is syrupy. Remove from heat. Strain mixture through a fine sieve over a jug. Discard solids. Wash and dry pan. Return syrup to pan. Bring to a simmer over medium heat. Simmer for 5 minutes or until slightly thickened. Add strawberries. Cook for 2-3 minutes or until strawberries are just beginning to soften. Remove from heat. Set aside for 10 minutes to cool.

3 Meanwhile, preheat a waffle maker. Combine the flour and sugar in a large bowl. Make a well. Whisk eggs, milk, butter and vanilla in a large jug. Gradually add the milk mixture to the flour mixture, whisking until almost smooth. Fold in the peanut butter chips.

4 Half-fill the waffle maker with batter. Close the lid. Cook for 1-2 minutes or until golden and cooked through. Transfer to wire rack in oven to keep warm. Repeat with remaining batter in 3 more batches.

5 Dust waffles with icing sugar. To serve, top with ice-cream, drizzle over the berry sauce and sprinkle with nuts.

NUTRITION (PER SERVE)

CALS	FAT	SAT FAT	PROTEIN	CARBS
566	28g	18g	15g	62g

○ FREEZABLE ● KID FRIENDLY ○ MAKE AHEAD ○ SPEEDY ● VEGO

CARAMEL DOUBLE-CHOC WAFFLES

This rich dessert is a sophisticated version of a caramel chocolate bar. Popular with kids or perfect with an after-dinner digestif or coffee.

SERVES 8 **PREP** 15 mins **COOK** 30 mins

200g dark chocolate, chopped
50g butter, chopped
2 eggs
330ml (1⅓ cups) milk
1 tsp vanilla extract
225g (1½ cups) self-raising flour
2 tbs cocoa powder
2 tbs caster sugar
250ml (1 cup) thickened cream, whipped, to serve
Grated dark chocolate, to serve

VANILLA CARAMEL SAUCE
100g (½ cup firmly packed) brown sugar
40g butter
½ tsp vanilla extract
125ml (½ cup) thickened cream

1 Preheat the oven to 150°C/130°C fan forced. Place a wire rack over a baking tray and place in the oven.

2 For the vanilla caramel sauce, place the sugar, butter, vanilla and cream in a medium saucepan over medium heat. Cook, stirring occasionally, for 5 minutes or until the butter has melted and sugar has dissolved. Bring to the boil. Reduce heat to low. Simmer for 10 minutes or until sauce is slightly thickened. Remove from heat.

3 Preheat a waffle maker. Place the chocolate and butter in a large microwave-safe bowl. Microwave on medium (50%), stirring with a metal spoon halfway through, for 2 minutes or until melted and smooth. Set aside for 5 minutes to cool slightly.

4 Whisk the eggs, milk and vanilla in a large jug. Gradually add to chocolate mixture, stirring until smooth and combined. Sift in the flour and cocoa. Add the sugar and whisk until almost smooth.

5 Half-fill the waffle maker with batter. Close the lid. Cook for 1-2 minutes or until cooked through. Transfer to wire rack in oven to keep warm. Repeat with remaining batter.

6 Transfer waffles to serving plates, dollop with whipped cream and drizzle with a little sauce. Sprinkle with chocolate and serve with remaining sauce.

NUTRITION (PER SERVE)

CALS	FAT	SAT FAT	PROTEIN	CARBS
604	39g	25g	9g	54g

○ FREEZABLE   ● KID FRIENDLY   ○ MAKE AHEAD   ○ SPEEDY   ● VEGO

15
minutes
prep

LEMON MERINGUE WAFFLE
SANDWICHES

Squish soft meringue and gooey lemon curd between
coconut waffles for a deliciously easy dessert.

SERVES 10 **PREP** 30 mins **COOK** 20 mins

2 eggs, separated
125ml (½ cup) milk
50g butter, melted
1 tsp finely grated lemon rind
100g (⅔ cup) self-raising flour
2 tbs desiccated coconut
1 tbs caster sugar
180g (⅔ cup) lemon curd
Icing sugar, for dusting
MERINGUE
150g (¾ cup) caster sugar
2 egg whites
Pinch of cream of tartar

1 Preheat oven to 150°C/130°C fan forced. Place a wire rack over a baking tray and place in oven.

2 Preheat a waffle maker. Whisk egg yolks, milk, butter and lemon rind in a large bowl. Whisk in flour, coconut and sugar until almost smooth. Using an electric mixer, beat egg whites in a bowl until stiff peaks form. Add a quarter of egg white to the coconut mixture, folding to combine. Add remaining egg white. Fold to combine.

3 Pour ⅓ cup batter into the waffle maker. Close the lid. Cook for 1 minute 30 seconds or until golden and cooked through. Use a knife to separate waffles into 5 small hearts. Transfer to wire rack in oven to keep warm. Repeat with remaining batter in another 3 batches to make 20 small waffle hearts.

4 For the meringue, place sugar and 60ml (¼ cup) water in a small heavy-based saucepan over low heat. Cook, stirring, for 3 minutes or until sugar dissolves. Increase heat to high. Bring to the boil. Boil, without stirring, for 5-6 minutes until mixture reaches hard ball stage (120°C on a candy thermometer).

5 Meanwhile, using an electric mixer on high speed, beat the egg whites and cream of tartar until soft peaks form. Reduce speed to low. Gradually add sugar syrup until just combined. Increase speed to high. Beat for 10-15 minutes until cooled and mixture becomes thick and glossy.

6 Spoon meringue onto half of the waffles on flat side. Using a kitchen blowtorch, lightly brown meringue. Top with lemon curd. Sandwich with remaining waffles. Dust with icing sugar. Serve immediately.

NUTRITION (PER SERVE)

CALS	FAT	SAT FAT	PROTEIN	CARBS
221	7g	4.4g	3.5g	36g

○ FREEZABLE ○ KID FRIENDLY ○ MAKE AHEAD ○ SPEEDY ● VEGO

VEGAN WAFFLES WITH CARAMEL

These gluten-free and dairy-free waffles are super simple with your waffle maker. Eat them hot or freeze them for later.

SERVES 8 **PREP** 15 mins **COOK** 30 mins

120g (⅔ cup) brown rice flour
125g (1 cup) arrowroot
2 tbs buckwheat flour
2½ tsp gluten-free baking powder
¼ tsp ground cinnamon
50g (¼ cup) coconut sugar
40g Nuttelex, melted, cooled
2 eggs substitute (see tip)
250ml (1 cup) soy milk
Dairy-free ice-cream, to serve
45g (¼ cup) roasted salted
   macadamias, chopped
Sliced banana, to serve

CARAMEL SAUCE
200g medjool dates, pitted
2 tbs coconut sugar
270g can light coconut cream
1 tsp vanilla bean paste

1 Preheat oven to 150°C/130°C fan forced. Place a wire rack over a baking tray and place in oven.

2 Sift the rice flour, arrowroot and buckwheat flour into a large bowl. Add the baking powder, cinnamon and coconut sugar. Stir until combined. Make a well in centre. Add Nuttelex, egg substitute and soy milk to well. Gradually whisk together until well combined and smooth.

3 Heat a waffle maker. Lightly spray with oil. Pour in ⅓ cup batter. Close the lid. Cook for 1-2 minutes until lightly golden and crisp. Transfer to wire rack in oven to keep warm. Repeat with remaining batter in 7 more batches

4 For the caramel sauce, combine the dates and 250ml (1 cup) water in a saucepan over medium heat. Simmer for 5 minutes or until softened. Add coconut sugar. Cook, stirring, for 2 minutes or until sugar dissolves. Add coconut cream and vanilla. Simmer, stirring, for 2-3 minutes, until dates break down and mixture is a golden caramel. Remove from heat and use a stick blender to puree until smooth.

5 Serve waffles with ice-cream and caramel sauce, and scattered with macadamia and banana.

COOK'S TIPS

Substitute gluten free cornflour for the arrowroot, if you prefer. There are a few different brands of egg substitute on the market. Whichever you choose, make the amount equivalent to 2 regular eggs.

NUTRITION (PER SERVE)

CALS	FAT	SAT FAT	PROTEIN	CARBS
505	21g	9g	6g	74g

● FREEZABLE   ○ KID FRIENDLY   ● MAKE AHEAD   ○ SPEEDY   ● VEGO

SWAP IT OUT
Need this recipe to be nut-free?
Swap out the macadamias for toasted coconut flakes.

WAFFLE-MAKER
HASH BROWNS

The ever-popular potato breakfast side is perfect with a hearty cooked meal of tomato and bacon and all your morning favourites.

SERVES 6 **PREP** 20 mins **COOK** 30 mins

1kg desiree potatoes, peeled
4 green shallots, thinly sliced
2 garlic cloves, crushed
2 tbs chopped fresh
   continental parsley
1½ tbs Dijon mustard
40g (¼ cup) self-raising flour
1 tsp sea salt
2 eggs, lightly beaten
60ml (¼ cup) milk
200g streaky bacon
2 tbs brown sugar
1 tbs maple syrup
2 x 310g pkts gem truss tomatoes
100g baby rocket
½ cup quark, to serve
Extra virgin olive oil, to serve

1 Preheat a waffle maker. Coarsely grate potato. Use hands to squeeze as much liquid from the potato as possible. Place in a bowl. Add shallot, garlic, parsley, mustard, flour, salt, egg and milk. Season with pepper. Stir to combine.

2 Spoon 2 tablespoons of batter onto each half of the waffle maker. Close the lid. Cook for 3 minutes or until golden and cooked through. Transfer to a wire rack set over a baking tray and cover to keep warm. Repeat with remaining batter to make 18 small waffles in total.

3 Meanwhile, preheat the oven to 200°C/180°C fan forced. Line 2 large baking trays with baking paper.

4 Place a wire rack over 1 prepared tray. Place bacon, in a single layer, on the wire rack. Combine sugar and maple syrup in a bowl. Brush onto the bacon. Bake for 15 minutes, brushing bacon with maple syrup mixture every 5 minutes.

5 Place tomatoes on remaining prepared tray. Spray with oil and season. Place in oven with the bacon. Bake for 15 minutes, brushing bacon with maple syrup mixture every 5 minutes, or until bacon is golden and sticky, and tomatoes are beginning to collapse.

6 Arrange waffles, tomatoes, bacon and rocket on a serving platter. Serve with quark drizzled in oil and seasoned with pepper.

NUTRITION (PER SERVE)

CALS	FAT	SAT FAT	PROTEIN	CARBS
336	14g	6g	16g	34g

○ FREEZABLE ● KID FRIENDLY ○ MAKE AHEAD ○ SPEEDY ○ VEGO

SWEET BREAKFAST OAT CAKES

All the goodness of oats is cooked into these pretty waffles.
Serve with yoghurt and berry compote for a sweet brekkie treat.

SERVES 6 **PREP** 15 mins **COOK** 25 mins

340g (2¼ cups) self-raising flour
50g (½ cup) instant oats
70g (⅓ cup) caster sugar
4 eggs
580ml (2⅓ cups) milk
160g butter, melted, cooled
2 tsp vanilla extract
130g (½ cup) plain Greek-style
  yoghurt, to serve

BLUEBERRY & ELDERFLOWER COMPOTE

1 vanilla bean, split
225g (1⅓ cups) caster sugar
60ml (¼ cup) elderflower cordial
500g frozen blueberries

1 Preheat oven to 150°C/130°C fan forced. Place a wire rack over baking tray and place in oven.

2 Preheat a waffle maker. Combine flour, oats and sugar in a bowl. Make a well in the centre. Whisk eggs, milk, butter and vanilla in a jug. Gradually add egg mixture to well, whisking until almost smooth.

3 Pour ⅓ cup of batter into the waffle maker. Close the lid. Cook for 1-2 minutes until golden and cooked through. Transfer to wire rack in the oven to keep warm. Repeat with remaining batter to make 12 oat cakes.

4 Meanwhile, to make the compote, use a knife to scrape vanilla seeds from bean. Place vanilla seeds and pod, sugar, cordial and 250ml (1 cup) water in a medium saucepan over medium heat. Cook, stirring, for 2-3 minutes or until sugar has dissolved. Bring to the boil. Reduce heat to low. Simmer for 8 minutes or until slightly thickened. Add the blueberries. Simmer for 10 minutes or until blueberries start to collapse.

5 Serve the oak cakes warm topped with yoghurt and drizzled in blueberry and elderflower compote.

NUTRITION (PER SERVE)

CALS	FAT	SAT FAT	PROTEIN	CARBS
838	32g	19g	16g	124g

○ FREEZABLE ● KID FRIENDLY ○ MAKE AHEAD ○ SPEEDY ● VEGO

15
minutes
prep

233

CARAMELISED MANDARIN BROWNIES

These are not your everyday brownies. The deliciously tangy mandarin topping and rich chocolate sauce make them something special.

SERVES 6 **PREP** 25 mins (+ 4 hours chilling) **COOK** 40 mins

125g dark chocolate chips
125g unsalted butter, chopped
2 eggs, lightly whisked
80ml (⅓ cup) milk
150g (1 cup) plain flour
155g (¾ cup firmly packed)
  brown sugar
1½ tsp baking powder
Pinch of salt
Chocolate ice-cream, to serve
MANDARIN COMPOTE
215g (1 cup) caster sugar
125ml (½ cup) water
5 mandarins, peeled, sliced
  crossways
CHOCOLATE SAUCE
300ml pouring cream
100g dark chocolate chips

1 For the mandarin compote, place sugar and water in a saucepan over medium heat. Cook, stirring, until sugar dissolves. Bring to the boil. Simmer, without stirring, for 15 minutes or until mixture turns a deep caramel. Stir in mandarin. Remove from heat. Cool. Place in the fridge for 4 hours or overnight, to develop the flavours.

2 For the sauce, place the cream and chocolate in a microwave-safe bowl. Microwave, stirring every 30 seconds, until melted and smooth. Set aside.

3 Place the chocolate and butter in a heatproof bowl over a saucepan of simmering water (don't let bowl touch the water). Stir with a metal spoon until melted. Remove from heat. Quickly stir in egg, milk, flour, sugar, baking powder and salt until just combined. Pour into a jug.

4 Preheat a waffle maker. Pour in ½ cup of batter. Close the lid. Cook for 2-3 minutes until cooked through. Carefully use a flat-bladed knife to loosen waffle and slide onto a plate (waffle will be soft). Cover with a tea towel to keep warm. Repeat with remaining batter to make 6 waffles. Serve with compote, ice-cream and chocolate sauce.

NUTRITION (PER SERVE)

CALS	FAT	SAT FAT	PROTEIN	CARBS
986	54g	34g	10g	120g

○ FREEZABLE ● KID FRIENDLY ○ MAKE AHEAD ○ SPEEDY ● VEGO

RAINBOW WAFFLE
STACK

Make the ultimate kids' party dessert in less than half an hour, with nothing more than basic waffle batter and food colouring.

MAKES 12 **PREP** 20 mins **COOK** 15 mins

450g (3 cups) self-raising flour
1 tsp bicarbonate of soda
1½ tbs caster sugar
435ml (1¾ cups) milk
3 eggs
90g butter, melted
6 different food colourings (see tip)
Ice-cream, to serve
Maple syrup, to serve

1 Preheat oven to 150°C/130°C fan forced. Place a wire rack over baking tray and place in oven.

2 Peheat a waffle maker. Sift the flour and bicarb into a large bowl. Stir in the sugar and make a well. Add milk, eggs and butter to well. Gradually whisk until well combined.

3 Divide the waffle batter among 6 bowls. Add a different food colouring to each bowl, adding a few drops at a time and stirring until mixture is vibrant in colour.

4 Spoon each portion of batter into a separate piping or sealable plastic bag. Cut end or corner off each bag and stand upright in a glass.

5 Working quickly, pipe the first coloured mixture in a ring about 2cm from the edge of the waffle maker. Pipe a different coloured ring inside the first ring. Repeat, using different colours, to make 4-5 rings. Close the lid. Cook for 1 minute or until cooked through. Transfer waffle to wire rack in oven to keep warm. Repeat with the remaining mixtures, alternating colours for each waffle, to make 12.

6 Stack waffles on a serving plate. Top with ice-cream and drizzle with maple syrup to serve.

COOK'S TIP

We used Wilton Icing Colours concentrated pastes in Red, Violet, Sky Blue, Golden Yellow, Rose and Leaf Green.

NUTRITION (EACH)

CALS	FAT	SAT FAT	PROTEIN	CARBS
293	11g	7g	8g	40g

○ FREEZABLE ● KID FRIENDLY ○ MAKE AHEAD ○ SPEEDY ● VEGO

CHICKEN & AVOCADO
CAESAR

Toast up a waffle as a base for a delicious salad and add chicken and homemade caesar salad dressing for authentic flavour.

SERVES 4 **PREP** 20 mins **COOK** 10 mins

300g (2 cups) self-raising flour
Pinch salt
2 eggs
435ml (1¾ cups) milk
80ml (⅓ cup) vegetable oil
50g (⅔ cup) finely grated parmesan
1 baby cos lettuce, shredded
½ barbecued chicken, meat and skin
   shredded, bones removed
1 avocado, sliced
4 rashers short cut bacon, cooked
   until crisp, chopped
Micro herbs, to serve
Lemon wedges (optional), to serve
CAESAR SALAD DRESSING
85g (⅓ cup) whole egg mayonnaise
2 anchovy fillets, finely chopped
1 tbs fresh lemon juice
½ tsp Worcestershire sauce

1 For the dressing, whisk all the ingredients together in a bowl until smooth. Set aside.

2 Sift flour and salt into a large bowl. Make a well. Whisk eggs, milk and oil in a jug. Add to the well and use a whisk to gently stir to combine. Stir in half the parmesan.

3 Preheat oven to 100°C/80°C fan forced. Place a wire rack over a baking tray and place in the oven.

4 Preheat a waffle maker and spray the top and bottom lightly with oil. Spread ⅓ cup batter over the base of each hole. Close the lid. Cook for 2 minutes or until golden. Transfer waffle to the wire rack in the oven to keep warm. Repeat to make 2 more plain waffles. Use remaining mixture to make 4 more waffles, sprinkling 1 tablespoon of the remaining parmesan over each waffle after cooking, then cooking for a further 1 minute until the cheese is melted.

5 Place 1 plain and 1 cheese waffle on each serving plate. Top with the lettuce, chicken, avocado and bacon. Drizzle with the dressing. Sprinkle with micro herbs and serve with lemon wedges, if using.

COOK'S TIP

Use 80ml (⅓ cup) bought Caesar salad dressing, instead of making your own, if you prefer.

NUTRITION (PER SERVE)

CALS	FAT	SAT FAT	PROTEIN	CARBS
1131	24g	14g	68g	63g

○ FREEZABLE ○ KID FRIENDLY ○ MAKE AHEAD ● SPEEDY ○ VEGO

BREAKFAST HASH
ROSTIS

Use your waffle maker to create an easy potato rosti with just two ingredients, then add chorizo, eggs and salad for a full breakfast.

SERVES 4 **PREP** 20 mins **COOK** 15 mins

4 x 250g sebago potatoes, peeled, halved

2 tbs chopped fresh chives, plus extra, to serve

2 chorizo, sliced

4 eggs

2 avocado, sliced

Mixed cherry tomatoes, halved, to serve

Mixed salad leaves, to serve

HP Sauce, to serve

1 Preheat oven to 150°C/130°C fan forced. Place potato in a saucepan and cover with cold water. Place over medium heat. Cover and bring to the boil. Uncover and boil for 5 minutes or until the potato is partially cooked (it should be cooked on the outside, but starchy and sticky on the inside). Transfer to a plate and set aside until cool enough to handle.

2 Coarsely grate potato into a large bowl. Add the chives and season. Use your hands to mix until well combined.

3 Preheat oven to 100°C/80°C fan forced. Spray top and bottom of a waffle maker generously with oil. Place 1 cup of potato mixture in each hole and use damp fingertips to spread out evenly. Close the lid and turn on the waffle maker. Cook for 7 minutes or until golden. Turn off waffle maker and gently transfer to a plate. Place in the oven to keep warm. Repeat with the remaining potato mixture to make 4 waffles in total.

4 Meanwhile, heat a non-stick frying pan over medium heat. Add chorizo and cook, turning halfway, for 4 minutes or until golden. Transfer to a plate. Crack eggs into pan. Cook for 3 minutes for sunny-side up or until cooked to your liking.

5 Divide hash rostis among serving plates. Top with avocado, eggs, chorizo, tomato and salad leaves. Drizzle with sauce. Serve sprinkled with extra chives.

NUTRITION (PER SERVE)

CALS	FAT	SAT FAT	PROTEIN	CARBS
497	34g	9g	24g	20g

○ FREEZABLE ● KID FRIENDLY ○ MAKE AHEAD ○ SPEEDY ○ VEGO

HEALTHY HACK
*Use gluten-free chorizo and omit the HP sauce
for a gluten-free version of this recipe.*

MIDDLE EASTERN-STYLE FELAFFLES

What do you get when you combine felafel with waffles?
Felaffles! Try this quick and easy dish for lunch.

MAKES 3 **PREP** 5 mins **COOK** 25 mins

400g can chickpeas, rinsed, drained
50g (⅓ cup) plain flour
½ tsp baking powder
¼ cup chopped fresh continental
  parsley leaves, plus extra
  leaves, to serve
2 garlic cloves, chopped
1 tsp ground coriander
1 tsp ground cumin
½ tsp sea salt flakes
Labneh, sliced cherry tomatoes,
  thinly sliced radish, fresh mint
  leaves, lemon thyme sprigs and
  sliced chilli, to serve
Olive oil, to drizzle

1 Place chickpeas, flour, baking powder, parsley, garlic, coriander, cumin, salt and 125ml (½ cup) water in a food processor. Process until smooth.

2 Preheat a waffle maker and spray with oil. Spread one-third of the mixture over the base. Close the lid. Cook for 7 minutes or until crisp and golden. Repeat to make 3 waffles in total.

3 Top waffles with labneh, tomato, radish, mint, lemon thyme, chilli and extra parsley. Drizzle with olive oil and season to serve.

NUTRITION (EACH)

CALS	FAT	SAT FAT	PROTEIN	CARBS
289	13g	3.1g	10g	27g

COOK'S TIP

Top with tabouli bought from the deli section of the supermarket, instead of the mint and radish salad, if you prefer.

○ FREEZABLE ○ KID FRIENDLY ○ MAKE AHEAD ● SPEEDY ● VEGO

HEALTHY HACK

For a gluten-free version, use chickpea flour and gluten-free baking powder.

CHEESE, BACON &

ZUCCHINI

Savoury waffles are a great lunch alternative. Just like your favourite zucchini slice, this delicious dish is cooked in minutes.

MAKES 4 **PREP** 5 mins **COOK** 25 mins

150g zucchini, coarsely grated
2 eggs
50g grated cheddar
40g (¼ cup) self-raising flour
25g bacon, finely chopped
½ small brown onion, finely chopped
1 tbs olive oil
Mixed leaves and lemon wedges,
  to serve

1 Preheat a waffle maker. Combine all ingredients except the leaves and lemon in a large bowl. Season with pepper.

2 Pour one-third of the zucchini mixture into the waffle maker. Close the lid. Cook for 5-6 minutes until golden and cooked through. Repeat with the remaining mixture to make 3 more waffles.

3 Serve immediately with mixed leaves and lemon wedges to squeeze over.

COOK'S TIP

Keep in an airtight container in the fridge for up to 2 days. Reheat under a grill or in a toaster when ready to serve.

NUTRITION (EACH)

CALS	FAT	SAT FAT	PROTEIN	CARBS
155	9g	2.6g	10g	9g

★★★★★ *New brekkie fave. Serve with avo, sweet chilli sauce and spinach leaves. Yum. Quick and easy.* **PEAJAY2U**

● FREEZABLE ○ KID FRIENDLY ● MAKE AHEAD ● SPEEDY ○ VEGO

USE OUR HANDY INDEX FOR EVERYTHING YOU NEED
TO KNOW FROM KEY GUIDES TO MEAL FINDERS.

Pie Maker & Co
ALPHABETICAL INDEX

Looking for a favourite recipe? Here's a list of every recipe in this book
to make it easier to find the ones you want to cook again and again.

Pie Maker & Co

INDEX BY KEY GUIDE

Whether you want a freezable, make-ahead recipe, a kid-friendly snack, a speedy dinner or a hearty vegetarian meal, you'll find it here.

Pie Maker & Co
INDEX BY MEAL TYPE

From simple breakfast toasties to lavish desserts, we've got something
for every meal of the day and snacks in between.

BREAKFAST

Bacon-wrapped brekkie sandwich	170
Breakfast hash rostis	240
Cheesy corn fritters	50
Cheesy maple bacon jaffle	180
Cheesy potato & bacon bites	40
Easy breakfast frittatas	68
Easy brekkie toastie	194
Fluffy berry pancakes	52
Sugar-crust blueberry pancakes	38
Sweet breakfast oat cakes	232
Waffle-maker hash browns	230

LUNCH

10-minute bean tortillas	208
Black bean quesadillas	70
Cheese, bacon & zucchini	244
Cheesy corn fritters	50
Cheesy pesto & veg flatbreads	198
Cheesy truss tomato tarts	66
Chicken & avocado caesar	238
Chicken & sesame satay	200
Five-ingredient lasagne rolls	118
Greek-style chicken yiros	190
Ham & French onion toasties	56
Ham, cheese & garlic bread stacks	178
Hearty classic meat pies	86
Low-cal spicy vego triangles	204
Middle Eastern-style felaffles	242
Mini impossible quiches	74
Mini Mexican toasted bites	188
Quick chicken fried rice	146
Quick chipotle chicken wraps	206
Roasted vegetables on Turkish	212
Spinach & three-cheese pies	78
Toasted corned beef reuben	210
Toasted salmon burritos	186
Tuna & sweet corn melts	172
Zucchini & haloumi fritters	136

DINNER

Cheesy pesto & veg flatbreads	198
Crumbed chicken tenders	148
Five-a-day vegie quesadillas	176
Four-cheese calzones	76
Greek-style chicken yiros	190
Healthier Southern chicken	138
Hearty classic meat pies	86
Indian-spiced cauliflower	160
Kale, feta & fried egg quesadilla	202

Maple mustard pork belly	144
Mexican-style vegie tortillas	196
Pork & cabbage dim sims	116
Quick chicken fried rice	146
Roasted vegetables on Turkish	212
Speedy toasted beef tacos	192
Super-easy, cheesy pizzas	174
Toasted salmon burritos	186
Tomato & cheese tarts	134
Ultimate roast pork jaffle, the	184
Vegetarian pumpkin schnitzel	142
Vegie korma curry pies	62
Zucchini & haloumi fritters	136

SNACKS & SIDES

Apple & custard doughnuts	58
Apple custard teacakes	42
Apricot chicken dippers	112
Black bean quesadillas	70
Broccoli & bacon croquettes	162
Caramilk custard doughnuts	30
Cheese & ham waffle stack	216
Cheesecake swirl brownies	106
Cheesy corn fritters	50
Cheesy garlic bread bombs	90
Cheesy maple bacon jaffle	180
Cheesy potato & bacon bites	40
Cheesy truss tomato tarts	66
Choc-drizzled churros	220
Choc-hazelnut filled doughnuts	64
Chocolate & zucchini bites	100
Condensed milk muffins	60
Corn chip crumbed haloumi	158
Cream cheese-iced gingerbread	84
Crumbed chicken tenders	148
Easy banana muffins	150
Easy haloumi fingers	110
Five-ingredient lasagne rolls	118
Four-cheese calzones	76
Four-ingredient banana muffins	72
Four-ingredient brownie	140
French-fried zucchini	132
Frittatas with instant noodles	82
Ham, cheese & garlic bread stacks	178
Hearty classic meat pies	86
Lemon jelly cakes	102
Lemon squash scones	54
Meatball pizza subs	114
Mexican-style sausage rolls	164
Mini impossible quiches	74

Mini Mexican toasted bites	188
Pina colada tarts	32
Pork & cabbage dim sims	116
Raspberry & Nutella scrolls	48
Smoky chipotle chicken empanadas	152
Spinach & feta gozleme (pie maker)	80
Spinach & feta gozleme (sausage roll maker)	120
Spinach & three-cheese pies	78
Tomato & cheese tarts	134
Tuna & sweet corn melts	172
Wagon-wheel cookies	34
Zucchini slice muffins	88

DESSERT

Apple & custard doughnuts	58
Apple custard teacakes	42
Berry apple star tarts	98
Caramel double-choc waffles	224
Caramelised mandarin & brownies	234
Cheesecake swirl brownies	106
Choc-hazelnut filled doughnuts	64
Chocolate eclairs	124
Condensed milk muffins	60
Condensed milk ripple desserts	104
Cream cheese-iced gingerbread	84
Custard & apple pies	122
Easiest-ever creamy vanilla slice	128
Easy individual cherry pies	94
Easy jaffle-maker apple pie	182
Ferrero Rocher bombs	46
Irish cream brioche puddings	36
Lemon delicious puddings	96
Lemon jelly cakes	102
Lemon meringue waffle sandwiches	226
Lemon ricotta dessert cake	166
Neapolitan cakes	44
Nutella & custard parcels	214
Pancake-wrapped Mars Bars	126
Peanut butter berry waffles	222
Pina colada tarts	32
Puddings with molten chocolate	92
Rainbow waffle stack	236
Raspberry & Nutella scrolls	48
Vegan waffles with caramel	228

CREDITS

editor-in-chief Brodee Myers
brodee.myerscooke@news.com.au
group commissioning editor Cassie Gilmartin
food director Michelle Southan
book food editor Tracy Rutherford
magazine food editors Alison Adams, Gemma Luongo
creative director Giota Letsios
art director Natasha Barisa
book subeditors Melody Lord, Lynne Testoni
design concept Rachelle Napper, Brush Media
book art director Sarah Cooper
nutrition editor Chrissy Freer
editorial coordinator Elizabeth Hayes

director of FoodCorp Fiona Nilsson

HarperCollins*Publishers* Australia
publishing director Brigitta Doyle
head of Australian non-fiction Helen Littleton

CONTRIBUTORS

Recipes

Alison Adams, Cynthia Black, Claire Brookman,
Kim Coverdale, Ross Dobson, Chrissy Freer, Liz Macri,
Lucy Nunes, Kerrie Ray, Tracy Rutherford,
Michelle Southan, Katrina Woodman

Photography

Guy Bailey, Vanessa Levis, Nigel Lough, Amanda McLauchlan,
Mark O'Meara, Al Richardson, Jeremy Simons, Brett Stevens,
Craig Wall, Ian Wallace, Andrew Young

HarperCollins*Publishers*

Australia • Brazil • Canada • France • Germany • Holland
• Hungary • India • Italy • Japan • Mexico • New Zealand
• Poland • Spain • Sweden • Switzerland • United Kingdom
• United States of America

First published in Australia in 2021
by HarperCollins*Publishers* Australia Pty Limited
ABN 36 009 913 517
harpercollins.com.au

Copyright © NewsLifeMedia 2021

This work is copyright. Apart from any use as permitted
under the *Copyright Act 1968*, no part may be reproduced,
copied, scanned, stored in a retrieval system, recorded, or
transmitted, in any form or by any means, without the prior
written permission of the publisher.

A catalogue record for this book is available
from the National Library of Australia

ISBN 978 1 4607 5913 4 (paperback)
ISBN 978 1 4607 1288 7 (ebook)

Colour reproduction by Splitting Image Colour Studio,
Clayton Victoria
Printed and bound in China by 1010 Printing International
Limited

8 7 6 5 4 3   21 22 23

THANK YOU

At taste.com.au HQ, we love a good gadget – and creating delicious (and unexpected) meals using them! *Pie Maker & Co* is a cookbook that will allow you to have fun with your favourite kitchen appliances and create great family meals and delicious treats. We'd like to thank everyone on the Taste team who contributed to this book – from our foodies to photographers, stylists, designers, subeditors and the digital team. Each recipe is a result of their amazing passion and teamwork.

A huge thank you as well to Brigitta Doyle and Helen Littleton, our partners at HarperCollins. We're very thankful for your expertise and support.

We'd also like to thank... you, the audience of taste.com.au! Thousands of passionate cooks visit our site every day to plan, cook and share their reviews, ratings and recipe twists and tips. We love hearing about your passion for cooking and the gusto with which you make our recipes, so keep those reviews, comments and photos coming.